T0322656

Praise for *The Infertile Midwife*

'A vital, heartfelt read for anyone navigating the rough seas of infertility and pregnancy loss' **Leah Hazard**

'I read Sophie's words with tears, a lump in my throat, much nodding and laughter too. This beautifully written, tender book has captured so much of what I experienced and, when women share, it's incredibly comforting and empowering. I hope her book plays a part in the women's healthcare revolution that the world so needs' **Melissa Hemsley**

'Sophie's words provide a supportive lighthouse of hope for many. She is gifted at starting and facilitating the conversations, ensuring those who feel like they sit in the shadows of other people's celebrations are supported, seen and validated. She holds up a microphone to the stories that need to be heard, generously sharing her own along the way' **Anna Mathur**

'A book that is both heart-breaking and beautiful ... Sophie's book will be an invaluable source of comfort for anybody living through pregnancy or baby loss' **Pippa Vosper**

'A deeply personal account of infertility and loss, love and joy. I am so glad Sophie has shared the story of her three beautiful sons and I know it will help many, many readers. It was an honour to read this book.' **Marianne Levy**

'An important, insightful book for midwives and anyone interested in birth ... Well written, deeply personal [it's] a story that will resonate with many readers. This is an important story to tell and highlights, also, the importance of language used around birth' **Anna Kent**

'No one wants to have a story like this to tell. But Sophie does it with honesty and bravery. Heartache and hope jump off every page. She's given her little boys the centre stage they deserve. Hard to read at times but important that we do' **Gabriella Griffith, Big Fat Negative podcast**

'What Sophie experienced on her journey into motherhood is nothing short of remarkable, and it is such a privilege to be taken along on that journey through the pages of this brilliant book. Honest, heart-breaking, and funny; it had me nodding along, crying and laughing in equal measure ... I am just so glad it's here to support those who need it now' **Elle Wright**

the infertile midwife

In Search of Motherhood
A Memoir

sophie martin

Hardie Grant

QUADRILLE

Publishing Director Sarah Lavelle
Commissioning Editor Sarah Thickett
Cover Design Anna Morrison
Head of Design Katherine Case
Head of Production Stephen Lang
Production Controller Martina Georgieva

Published in 2023 by Quadrille, an imprint of
Hardie Grant Publishing

Quadrille
52–54 Southwark Street
London SE1 1UN
quadrille.com

The content of this book is the opinion of the
author and is not intended as a substitute for
professional medical advice, diagnosis or treatment.
Always seek the advice of a qualified health provider
with any questions you may have regarding a
medical condition.

To preserve patient confidentiality, names, events
and identifying characteristics have been changed.

Cataloguing in Publication Data: a catalogue record
for this book is available from the British Library.

Text © Sophie Martin 2023
Design © Quadrille 2023

ISBN 978 1 83783 064 0
Printed in the UK

To Cecil and Wilfred,
I'll spend a lifetime loving you.

Contents

Prologue

As James and I got into bed, I knew it would be a restless night. Over a year of waiting, months of hoping and weeks of injections had all led up to this moment. Every day of the past two weeks had dragged – I could feel every single second as it passed. On waking, we would know whether our gamble had paid off, or whether we would be picking ourselves up, dusting ourselves off and starting again on our pursuit of parenthood.

I lay there for what felt like hours, tossing and turning, trying not to disturb James. I tried not to look at the clock, as that made the time pass even more slowly, but eventually I gave in. It was 2 a.m. Far too early to get up, so I rolled over and tried to ignore my heart, which was beating so loudly I thought the neighbours would hear.

Two hours later, I was unable to wait any longer. I turned over and asked James whether it was finally time. I had felt my bladder filling overnight and, due to nerves, I could hold it no longer. He agreed that as neither of us was sleeping, we might as well get up.

I had left a pot out ready, alongside a pregnancy test. My eyes had to adjust to the light, as I carefully unwrapped the test and balanced it on the side of the bath. I then peed into the pot and dipped the tip of the test into it. I washed my hands and placed the test on the side of the basin. Unable to sit and watch, I climbed back into bed to wait for those three long minutes. James set an alarm and we lay there counting down. Having done countless pregnancy tests over the years and never seeing a positive result before, this finally felt like we might have a chance. Despite knowing that the chances of IVF working are around 30 per cent each cycle, the fact that doctors were involved made it feel like we might be successful.*

During those three minutes I imagined the two outcomes that were facing us. It felt like a *Sliding Doors* moment, with our lives about to change drastically regardless. A positive result meant we had the chance of a family. There might be a microscopically small person who was making a little home inside me. We could finally move on to the next stage of our lives and become parents together. I imagined family holidays and grubby hands and smiling, laughing faces.

Or the test would be a stark negative. We would have to start all over again, finding yet more money to afford another chance at a baby. We would have to pick ourselves up, dust ourselves off, ignore the emotional bruises and soldier on. More injections, more financial sacrifices, more emotional heartache, all because we wanted a family.

I couldn't bear to think of the look on James' face if only one line on the test stared back at us. In my mind it was my fault we were in this situation, so to disappoint him all over again would break my heart. My rational brain knew that I had not caused my infertility, but I still blamed myself. I tried to push the thoughts of him putting on a brave face to the back of my mind. We would find a way to comfort each other and keep going.

We had been very private about our infertility struggles; in particular, I had kept this a secret from my colleagues at work. I am a midwife, and I felt ashamed that I wasn't able to get pregnant without help. However, we had recently confided in both sets of parents. I

---

* For an overview of how IVF works and the statistics involved, see: https://www.nhs.uk/conditions/ivf/

played the conversations over in my head, wondering how we might break the news either way. Having to call and share the news that, yet again, we were failing at making a family felt like an added insult. On the other hand, imagining sharing our success gave me a bubble of hope in my chest.

We had booked Official Test Day (as it is known in the fertility world) off work, so we could take time to process the news either way. I wasn't sure I could face going into work if it was negative. Having to plaster on a smile and coo over other people's babies, while my own womb remained like a void, did not seem appealing. Then we had booked to visit friends – hopefully a welcome distraction. IVF had controlled our lives for the past six weeks and being able to make plans felt like a luxury. If the result was negative, I was at least planning on having a large glass of wine.

Those three minutes seemed to last an eternity. The timer on James' phone eventually went off, and we both got up and walked into our bathroom, ready to see whether our hard-earned embryo had implanted into my womb. Despite counting down to this moment, all of a sudden I didn't want to see the result. I wasn't sure I would be able to face the disappointment if it was negative. James had never looked at a pregnancy test before and asked me what it meant. My shaking hands picked up the test, as I took a deep breath and looked.

Introduction

I have been a practising midwife for a number of years, but my journey to motherhood taught me more about my profession than any training or my years of work. Many midwives go on to be mothers, but far fewer go through infertility and loss. It is the experience of sitting on the other side of the consulting room that has provided me with levels of empathy I didn't have access to before.

This is my own personal account of living through infertility and baby loss while also practising as a midwife. It is a unique experience to be surrounded by the one thing you want more than anything in the world, a baby, knowing that it is just outside of your grasp. Being forced to sit with your childlessness while confronted with a stream of bumps and babies is no easy feat. Despite working within a system where, sadly, infertility and baby loss are familiar scenarios, I found that there is still a deep level of misunderstanding and sometimes ignorance when it comes to addressing these difficult and life-changing experiences.

I myself was guilty of underestimating how living through infertility and baby loss can really take a toll on a person. I can now say, looking back, that I lost myself for a number of years. Although motherhood should not characterise a person, I felt like my inability to be a mother defined me. It consumed my every thought, and I couldn't contemplate a life without a living child.

My sense of womanhood and my sense of self were so intertwined with my ability to reproduce. If I wasn't a mother then I wasn't worthy of womanhood. It saddens me that the primary narrative for women is one of motherhood. When women choose not to have children, or for whatever reason aren't able to be a parent, they are shifted from motherhood to otherhood.

There is no one way to be a woman, nor is there any one way to feel like a woman. It can seem as though stereotypes dominate the expectations for womanhood. We are often seen as nurturers and care givers, while men are more likely to be seen as breadwinners and providers. The majority of women do choose to have children. Others, for various circumstantial reasons, feel the choice is taken away from them. They may be in challenging relationships or not in a relationship at all and therefore unable to pursue the life they wish for. There are women who do have children and long for their pre-motherhood lives. There are also women who choose not to have children. What I want to discuss is another group: the women whose freedom to choose whether or not they become mothers is removed from them by their bodies.

Infertility and loss are not glamorous subjects. They are raw and painful, and not spoken about enough, whether it's due to feelings of shame or embarrassment, a fear of judgement or simply the challenge of processing your own feelings. I longed to speak to anyone who would understand how I was feeling. Not to mention the fact that I wanted talk about the yearning I felt alongside the physical impact of IVF.

While in the depths of my loneliness and despair at my failure to become a mother, I started seeking out other women online who'd had similar experiences. All of a sudden I found hundreds of others who understood how I was feeling. I immediately felt able to connect more with these complete strangers than I could with some of my own friends.

Initially, I set up an anonymous online account where I could talk about the experiences and emotions I was going through. The account grew more and more popular, and I decided to go public and share my experiences further. Being open with my story, and hearing those of other women, has been the single most helpful thing to me during my long road to motherhood.

Just as important, sharing my story and hearing the stories of others has had a huge impact on how I practise as a midwife, and in particular how I phrase things when speaking to women or colleagues. Language is incredibly important, especially within a healthcare setting. The traditional language of maternity services is set up for women; however, over recent years there has been a move to include all birthing people regardless of gender. Throughout this book I refer to mothers and women, unless otherwise stated, as I am speaking from my own perspective about my own experiences. I don't want to speak for communities that I am not part of, but I stand in solidarity with anyone who has had a more challenging route to parenthood, whatever that looks like. There are many ways to be a parent, all of which are valid and should be embraced.

It is hopefully already clear that this book will cover the details of my infertility story, alongside stories of baby loss. Writing about the hardest moments of my life was not easy, and I know that reading it may also have its challenges. Be gentle with yourself.

1

The Life Plan

I had always imagined that my life would follow a certain formula. An unspoken trajectory, following in the footsteps of my family and accompanied by my friends around me. Although the exact achievements might differ from person to person, it was clear to me from early on that ideally you grew up, got a job, got married and had children. There might be other notable occasions along the way, but as a child I knew that these were the milestones that lay ahead of me. Admittedly, this is quite a traditional pathway through life, but it was the message I had received from books, television and the media, and what I had seen in my own family growing up.

As I got older, and as I visualised more clearly the route my life would take, the Life Plan morphed slightly. Goals were adjusted, achievements were added, but the idea that I might not make it through this list never crossed my mind. It didn't seem possible that life could take any other format than the uncomplicated one that I saw all around me playing out through family, friends and the world I lived in. I didn't assume that everything would come easily to me – I knew I would have to work hard, but I was prepared to do so for a happy life. When on the brink of adulthood, I had my life mapped out, and it looked something like this:

Complete university degree (ideally with first-class honours)

Meet man of dreams (tall and handsome)

Move in with aforementioned dream man (trendy London flat if possible)

Get dream job (I hadn't managed to figure out exactly what that job would be just yet)

Get engaged (yellow-gold ring, with diamond halo)

White wedding (with lots of dancing and champagne)

Honeymoon (with social-media-worthy beach destination)

Buy house (complete with garden)

Birth three children (with two-year age gap in between each child)

Yearly holidays (to various photogenic destinations)

Live Happily Ever After

Despite my certainty that this fantasy would come true, I also acknowledged that there might be a few bumps along the road. Perhaps a break-up, or losing out on a job, from which I could rise from the ashes stronger and more resilient. I saw these as mere hiccups or inconveniences that would become good dinner-table chat in later years. Although I knew terrible things happened all around me, I assumed they couldn't, or wouldn't, happen to me. I now appreciate what an unbelievably privileged and cosseted view of the world I had. Even when I feel I have been taught one of the harshest life lessons on offer, I know that I am so lucky to have such fantastic support around me, along with stability in my home, family and relationships.

Having managed to sail through most of the list, in my late twenties I arrived firmly at a stalemate with my ovaries. I desperately wanted to be a mother, having dreamt of that moment from when I was a little girl playing with dolls, and now it might never happen.

Friends and family members all seemed to conceive and have babies with ease. And even if their story had been more complicated, it hadn't been shared so I was none the wiser. I'd not had even a hint of a positive pregnancy test. I was being left behind, while other people lapped me and brought home second and third children. The Life Plan had ground to a halt, and I couldn't see how to progress any further. I both hated myself for wanting to conform and yearned to fit in and be like everyone else. I began to wonder why I had believed so vehemently in this picture-perfect plan in the first place.

The rise of social media has made it easy to showcase a highlights reel of life. This in turn makes it clear that if you aren't hitting certain goals, then your life is surely lacking in comparison. I have often found myself scrolling through the nursery and newborn photographs of an old school acquaintance that I haven't spoken to in over ten years. This practice has led to intense distress, sadness and feelings of unworthiness. My inability to move forward has been exacerbated by the impression that I am being left behind. My peers appear to be merrily progressing in the Game of Life, while I can't even find my playing pieces yet. Ever since my fertility stumbling block, during which James and I tried for a baby and ended up undergoing countless fertility treatments, I have questioned where my life expectations came from. Why did I imagine I would have three children and live in the suburbs?

Our parents are our very first teachers. Much of infanthood requires copying those around us in order to learn those skills ourselves, such as speaking and walking. So it makes sense that we imagine our future lives from observing others around us. My parents met young, had children young, and are still happily married over thirty-five years later. My extended family of grandparents, aunts and uncles, all of whom similarly married early, also had children and remained together. Strong family values were an important part of my upbringing, and my extended family is close-knit, which is helped by us living in close proximity to one another near the coast in south Essex.

I am the eldest of three, with a younger brother and sister. As the eldest, it was drilled into me that I had to set an example to the younger two. I helped bath my baby brother when he was born and remember watching my mum breastfeed my baby sister when she arrived three years after him. Being the oldest also lent itself to my bossy, headstrong nature, which my siblings still like to remind me of. I had a content and comfortable childhood, and my parents tried their hardest to make sure that my siblings and I were safe, happy and loved.

My parents always say I was a determined and strong-willed child. If I set my sights on something, I was going to get there. During primary school, we would put on musical performances for our parents to watch at the end of the year. One year we were told that a girl would be picked to sing the solo in a performance of *Annie*. Naturally I came home and told my parents that I was going to be Annie before the auditions had even been announced. My singing voice has never been particularly stand-out, but with my trademark grit and determination, I managed to score the part.

Leading by example, my parents were firm believers in working hard. They instilled in us that we should always try our best and that if we applied ourselves, we would be able to achieve anything. Neither of my parents went to university, and they both had successful careers and were able to provide a fulfilling family life, with plenty of home comforts around us. The frustrating thing is that in my adult life, as hard as I tried to have a baby, the effort I put in never led to the desired outcome. It felt like my whole life had been a lie. Sometimes you try your hardest, and you are still left empty-handed.

My mum worked as a nurse and then a midwife during our early years, then after the birth of my sister she transitioned to being a full-time parent. Some early memories of mine involve my dad looking after my brother and me downstairs, trying to get us to play as quietly as possible, while my mum slept between her night shifts. My dad prospered by nurturing a business over the years. Their success was always attributed to working hard and persevering even when things were difficult.

It was always explained to me that if I went to the best school, then I would hopefully get good grades, which would lead to a good job and a happy life. At my all-girls grammar school, there was no mention of personal satisfaction from, say, a fulfilling relationship (or what that even entailed), or practical lessons on life skills such as finances or health. From an early age, it seemed life was mapped out in front of me, and it was purely achievement-based.

The standard expectation in grammar school was to excel. Although it was never articulated out loud, I felt a sense that only the very brightest students were valued. The teachers were kind, but it was considered a failure to get a C grade. I remember one year I got a D in history and felt a sense of complete and utter humiliation. I quickly decided that I never wanted to be at the bottom of the class again. I began to develop a fear of failure and threw myself into making sure I always achieved whatever was required.

Fortunately, through my dedication, I was able to achieve good grades, but my self-confidence was slightly battered in the ultra-competitive environment. Within my friendship group I always felt like I had to work a lot harder to achieve similar results to the others. Looking back, I can see how these heightened environments are not always the most helpful to the self-esteem of young girls.

Single-sex education does not suit everyone, but I didn't know any different and have mainly fond memories of school. I have always enjoyed the company of other girls or women. My school, my university degrees and now my career are near-exclusively female environments. Being able to relate to other women is something that I pride myself on, and sharing experiences with them really helps to strengthen the bonds between us. There is something incredibly magical that happens when women support each other. The camaraderie from shared experiences has always been a source of strength to me.

Surprisingly, motherhood was not really mentioned at school. Biology lessons were kept formal, so we learnt about the hormones of the menstrual cycle, but it was never explained how this related to real life. Sex education was almost non-existent, other than one particularly memorable PSHE lesson. Needless to say, fitting a condom onto a white plastic tube was very entertaining to a class full of fifteen-year-old girls. The idea that you could become pregnant from having sex once was widely talked about. I sometimes want to laugh when I think about the reality of how difficult it is for some people to have a baby when the rhetoric in our youth tells us exactly the opposite. There was no mention at all of infertility or miscarriage in any classes. The purpose of sex education was solely to prevent pregnancy. I was only too eager to learn how to avoid this, as teenage pregnancy was billed as a fate worse than death. I received absolutely no advice on how to plan and prepare for a pregnancy, and barely understood the inner workings of my own body. Given the academic focus of the schooling, we were encouraged to give all our attention to the immediate future of securing our place at university. A baby would come with ease at the time of our choosing.

When it came to selecting our career options, I'm sure like many teenagers I had little idea of what the future might hold. At school it was expected that I would go on to university. At home my parents wanted us to be happy and also successful. At school there was a heavy focus on the application process, and I'm sure it must have been very alienating for those who were considering other paths. There was a strong bias towards the girls who were likely to be accepted into Oxford or Cambridge, and I was not one of them. Despite not really knowing what I wanted to do in life, I was told my next step was to apply for university, so being the dutiful student, I happily went along with this plan.

At this time, I fleetingly toyed with the idea of becoming a midwife, as that had always been something I'd carried a torch for. I remembered going into the hospital to visit my mum on a few occasions. One of those days was when my dad had been looking after us while Mum was working. We were never allowed to play with balls inside, for fear of breaking something, but on this day my dad joined in with us. Not only were we breaking the rules, but my brother trod on the ball and slid over, cracking his head on a plant pot. I still remember the noise it made as the ceramic pot shattered. My dad then had to take us both to the hospital where my mum worked, so she could patch it up and put some stitches in my brother's head. Seeing my mum in her uniform, always looking so professional, being able to fix scrapes or cuts, was always so comforting. My teenage self quickly dismissed the idea that I could be a midwife, however, as I felt I wasn't clever enough, and at the time I had a fear of needles (which, luckily, I later outgrew). This seems particularly laughable now when I think about how many injections I've given myself over the years. I've even managed to take my own blood, all in the pursuit of having a baby.

Having been fortunate enough to have theatre and dance lessons throughout childhood, I decided to carry on with my favourite subjects without much thought for a career at the end of it all. As I had been taught, I assumed that if I worked hard enough, everything would work out for the best in the end.

Ultimately my decision not to become a midwife at that time led me to find the other half of my heart: my husband, James.

I met James at university in London when we were both aged nineteen. I was studying for a drama degree, and James was attempting an English and drama course. I wish our first meeting was more glamorous, but we were first introduced at the students' union bar through mutual friends. It was lust at first sight, aided by high levels of inebriation. I was impressed with James' posh Surrey accent and his floppy hair. I'm still not sure to this day what James saw in me, but I'm thankful that the stars aligned and we both decided to visit the bar that night.

James, the gentleman, walked me home, then headed across the road to his own flat. He added me on Facebook and we began chatting. The following weeks and months were a cat-and-mouse game, each showing the other increased attention, then retreating. I maintain that I knew straight away that I was serious about James, but he needed more convincing! As we were part of the same course, we socialised with our peers most nights, and were both in the university theatre company too.

It was when we started our second year of university that we became an official couple. After that, we fell into a happy existence of watching *The X Factor* on a Saturday night, practising our cooking and visiting Brick Lane at the weekends, alongside stumbling home from the very bar where we first met.

James showed far less commitment to his course than I did. He was a little too interested in extra-curricular activities, mainly the rugby club and the pub, and did not seem to be so driven to achieve as I was. In the end he dropped out of university after his second year. Following in his family's footsteps, he left his course and began working in hospitality. Since then, James has worked in many different pubs and restaurants, and it suits him down to the ground. He is so friendly and chatty and makes the perfect pub landlord. James is far more confident than me and finds it so easy to talk to strangers. I am the opposite, and often feel quite shy.

I do remember feeling a sense of dread when I had to break the news to my parents that James had dropped out. I really wanted them to like him and being a beauty-school drop-out did not exactly suggest great boyfriend material. Luckily, James had already charmed my mum, and if my parents were less than impressed, they never let on.

Although neither James nor I believe in fate or destiny, we are both in full agreement that the only reason we went to university was to meet each other. Neither of us work in the field we chose to study in, but we don't regret our choices for a second as they would not have led us to each other. We spoke early on about having a family and knew it was something we both wanted together.

Towards the end of my drama degree, I decided that I wanted to do a master's in theatre and performance. At the time I was focused on a career in the arts, possibly working for a theatre or theatre company. But almost as soon as I started the course, I realised I was out of my depth. Being the youngest person in all my classes, aged only twenty-one, I felt like a fraud. I struggled through the first term, often not understanding entire seminars. I would write down words I didn't understand, and then look up their meanings in the dictionary as soon as I got home. It started to feel like I had made a terrible mistake.

While the other course members seemed preoccupied with 'making a difference', I struggled to see what that meant in real terms. I grappled to see how sitting in our seminar room discussing gender politics would make a tangible difference to the lives of real people. I felt frustrated with all the theoretical discussions; I wanted to get out of the classroom and physically do something. I was also being drawn towards feminism and women's rights issues, with all the texts sounding like battle cries. I was learning about the struggles that women have faced throughout history, and still continue to face; how having children can stall a career for women, how women are unfairly penalised in the workplace and how equality is still just beyond our grasp. Ultimately, I wanted to be a better feminist. I didn't want to write or preach; I wanted to be among other women, doing whatever I could to support and empower them.

I realised that the reason my path had led me to study drama, at precisely the right moment in time, was to meet James. Now that we were committed to each other, I knew that my real vocation was to work with women. Deep down it felt like I had always wanted to be a midwife but had struggled with the confidence to go for it. Now was the time.

Ever the good student, I dutifully and painstakingly completed my master's. Having now done four years at university, I was slightly embarrassed at my change of career before my career had even started. Instead of feeling sorry for myself, I tried to see the positives and sought to bring my midwifery interests and influences into the course. I started researching the use of art and performance in hospitals and medical settings. I completed my thesis on Clown Doctors, which allowed me the privilege of watching Robin Williams star in *Patch Adams* guilt-free!

While James and I were dating, I explicitly said to him that I didn't want to move in with a boyfriend unless I thought I was going to marry them. It would not fit with the Life Plan to have a big break-up and have to separate all our shared belongings. James, to his credit, was unfazed by this and we set about searching for a flat to rent in South London, having grown tired of East London. We decided we would move in together once I had completed my master's. I think we had known all along that we were in this for the long haul.

Luckily, we discovered a one-bedroom flat in South-west London, which – compared to my four years in dingy student accommodation – felt like a cosy village. I felt so incredibly grown up, living with my boyfriend in London. We had a ground-floor flat with a small garden, and possibly the smallest kitchen I have ever seen – with barely enough room for one person to stand in there, let alone two. We loved cooking – still do – and considering the minuscule size of that kitchen, what we managed to produce in there was impressive. The most important thing was that it was ours.

Towards the end of my master's, I began to plan my next steps. I was reluctant to dive straight into a midwifery degree; it was embarrassing enough having to admit that after an undergraduate degree and a master's I wanted to start again from the beginning. I often wondered whether my desire to be a midwife was, in fact, a desire to be a mother. I didn't feel quite ready for motherhood; was this a stopgap until then? In order to make sure I was definitely making the right decision, I decided to try to gain some work in a maternity setting. Ultimately, it was the itch that I just had to scratch. I simply couldn't imagine doing anything else. I started applying for jobs as a maternity support worker (MSW) – the maternity version of a healthcare assistant. It finally felt like a step towards following my dream of becoming a midwife and allowed me to finish my course knowing that I had a plan in place. Although I had taken a few side steps, the Life Plan was still on track.

My mum had always spoken so favourably of her time working as a nurse and midwife – the camaraderie between colleagues and the special moments with new mums. She was incredibly supportive of me during this time, and knowing how kind and compassionate she was made me strive to be more like her. Some early memories of my mum include me sitting at her feet playing with a stethoscope while she blow-dried her hair before a night shift. Now I was going to need a stethoscope and would be staying up for night shifts of my own.

2

Call the Midwife

One way to learn about the world is to become a midwife. People from all walks of life have babies, so you are exposed to the entire spectrum of humanity in a maternity unit. There is no typical patient. Each woman who enters your care has a unique story to tell, and over the years I have found that I have learnt something from each patient I encounter.

Likewise, there is no typical midwife, as the role itself is very varied. Some midwives work in a community setting, based in a health centre or GP surgery. They will deliver antenatal care to women, attend homebirths in their areas, and then look after both mum and baby at home once the baby is born. Other midwives work in hospitals, based on wards. Typical wards include the antenatal clinic, antenatal ward, labour ward and postnatal ward. Again, there is no routine day in the life of a midwife, but it might include blood-pressure checks, taking blood, palpating a mother's abdomen to feel for the position of the baby, listening to the baby's heartbeat, supporting a mum during labour and birth, assisting with the birth of the placenta, performing any stitches required after birth, completing an initial inspection of a newborn baby, supporting a mother to breastfeed, running antenatal classes... the list could go on. The role is enormous, and it's often said that midwifery was one of the very first professions. For as long as humankind have had babies, there have been midwives in some capacity.

Having moved into the new flat with James and secured a job as a maternity support worker, I began settling into life on the maternity unit. I set about immersing myself in the maternity services and trying to learn as much as possible. An MSW is an unqualified worker who aids the midwives and the maternity department. Roles might include cleaning equipment, changing and making beds, and supporting mothers with breastfeeding. No formal training is required before applying to work as an MSW, and it provides plenty of opportunities to learn skills like taking blood, working in theatre, and taking mum and baby observations. I was ready for action: I had my bright-pink stethoscope, my freshly ironed scrubs, my Crocs and my endless determination. Perhaps having watched too many midwifery television programmes, I had somewhat rose-tinted expectations of life in maternity services. I knew that most of my mum's colleagues had left the profession due to dissatisfaction with the NHS, the long hours, the immense workload and the lack of breaks, but I was desperate to dive straight in.

Beginning work in a large hospital is always a baptism of fire, perhaps especially so in London. Unlike when I eventually became a student midwife (when there was a huge amount of support), as an MSW I was expected to be immediately proficient in the basic skills. After I started there were two short training days to teach me some very basic skills, such as taking blood pressure and heart rate, and checking urine samples; however, these didn't happen until a few weeks into the role, so those first few days I had absolutely no idea what I was doing. I was shocked that I was being let loose on patients without even the knowledge of basic observations. I was thankful that at university I had attended St John's Ambulance meetings and knew a little about basic first aid. On my very first day on the ward a midwife asked me to take a patient's blood pressure. I explained that I didn't know how to do that yet, but I was keen to learn if she would show me. Her reply of 'Why are you here if you can't do anything?' was deeply hurtful, and I questioned why I had started the job in the first place. Fortunately, this experience was a one-off. The rest of the staff members were lovely and helped me to settle in, teaching me the skills I needed to tide me over until the official training days began.

The only thing I knew how to do already was making beds. As a child, my mum never let us have fitted sheets, perhaps due to being a midwife herself, so I was already a seasoned professional at hospital corners well before I ever walked onto the ward. There is something so satisfying about making the perfect bed, and this was put to good use during my time on the postnatal ward. Twenty-seven beds, which needed to be changed and made every day – sometimes multiple times a day. Standing back and seeing those fresh, crisp sheets all tucked in felt like a great achievement, although the amount of bed-making was exhausting. This meant that I had very little energy for hospital corners by the time I finished work, so I allowed myself the luxury of fitted sheets at home!

Adjusting to shift work is not an easy task. Twelve and a half hours of being on your feet for the entirety is hard going. The night shifts I found particularly difficult, and ultimately, I learned that they played havoc with my hormones. Doing night shifts for the first time is always an experience – I remember crying for no reason on my first simply because I was overtired. It took me a while to adjust to eating at night-time, but after a few weeks of having banana and peanut butter bagels for every meal, I got into the swing of things. A full roast dinner at six o'clock in the morning? Not a problem. Breakfast at dinnertime? My favourite combination of meals!

In the hierarchy of the maternity unit, the MSW is at the bottom. The tasks I performed included cleaning, stocking, cleaning, taking blood, cleaning, working in the labour ward theatre counting swabs and instruments, supporting new mums with breastfeeding, taking observations – and did I mention cleaning?

It was an interesting contrast to my other work, as I was still studying for my master's at the same time. One day I would be reading Simone de Beauvoir and discussing women's rights; the next I would be scrubbing blood off the floor and fulfilling the tasks 'traditionally' assigned to women that the authors I was studying railed against. Although the work was far from glamorous, I got far more satisfaction from these physical tasks than I did from my studies. I felt part of something bigger. I knew that a kind word, or an offer of help, could make a lasting memory for a new mum, and that felt great.

My favourite part of the MSW role was when I was able to interact with patients. Any time when I could chat to them and find out about their lives was fascinating to me. On the postnatal ward I loved breastfeeding support. Mainly because this is not a job you can rush, so I would savour those moments when I could spend an hour with a new mum teaching her how to help her baby latch on to the breast – all the while learning about her life, her pregnancy, her feelings. When a baby finally latches, it is such a wonderful moment, and seeing how proud the new mum is of herself is always a pleasure to watch. When the midwives were busy doing other jobs or caring for other mothers, I loved being asked to help in some way, knowing that new mums would keenly take the support on offer.

The lives of these women were a treasure trove of unique experiences. Women who worked full time, women who had never worked, women who ran their own companies, women who looked after their children, women who were carers, single women – every kind of woman. In the particular area where I worked, the contrast between the most affluent and the poorest women was stark. The ward could be filled with women who were unlikely to ever meet each other outside of the hospital, their circumstances so different, and yet here they were, pregnant at the same time and being cared for side by side.

One time, staying on the antenatal ward in adjacent beds, were two women, both pregnant with their first baby, who couldn't have had more contrasting lives. The first woman had been trafficked to the UK from Syria and had suffered horrendously at the hands of her captors. She was in her early twenties, slim and attractive, with pretty good English. Somehow, she had escaped and made her way to A&E, where she was admitted and transferred to our ward. Now late in the pregnancy, and having received no antenatal care, she had no belongings at all and no place to go. She had no friends or relatives in the country, and it was unclear who the father of the baby was, or if she even knew. She remained as an inpatient for several days while accommodation was found for her, and social care was arranged to provide maximum support for the rest of the pregnancy. She smiled and laughed with all the staff. If I hadn't been aware of her story, I would never have guessed her circumstances. I was used to reading stories in the newspapers of the hardships that some people lived through, but seeing it play out in reality was shocking and eye-opening. Some days I realised that being a midwife was so much more than the medical aspect of the job. We were counsellors, social workers, hand holders, and so much more.

The second woman was being induced as her baby was overdue. As induction can be a long process, I checked in on her regularly. I saw she was busy on her laptop and I assumed she was distracting herself. After stopping for a brief chat, it transpired that she was still working. As she owned her own company and hadn't officially gone on maternity leave yet, she was trying to ignore her early contractions in between writing emails. In fact, she continued on her laptop for most of her labour; as it progressed, she received an epidural and was comfortable enough to prop her laptop up on a pillow. Hours after the baby was born, while breastfeeding, she was back on her phone making calls and typing emails. Single-handedly running her own company, and going home to a night nurse, she couldn't have been in a more different situation to her ward neighbour.

Neither woman knew the circumstances of the other. Perhaps they overheard snippets from their bed spaces, the doctors and midwives chatting during the ward round and so on. Their curtains remained closed around them, out of choice, as each wanted their privacy. Each focused on doing the best for their baby, oblivious to what was happening a few metres away from them. For me, the complex threads of these women's lives, interwoven with the commonality of pregnancy, led to a far greater understanding of feminism than any academic text could give me. Recognising the unique needs of a woman during her pregnancy is a skill that to this day I am still learning. I have never once regretted my career change, as having the opportunity to unashamedly focus on the needs of women is one of the greatest privileges I have ever been gifted.

Working as an MSW was an invaluable lesson, as it taught me kindness. I know what it feels like to be looked down on or spoken to rudely. Even now, I make sure I know the names of the cleaning staff and will make a point of saying hello. Everyone has vital roles within the team, and if you are kind to your colleagues and the staff members around you, then it is easier for them to be kind back. Most importantly, it means they have kindness to give to their patients. It costs nothing to smile and say hello, and yet sometimes we get caught up in our busy days and forget how transformative a friendly face can be. I consider this one of the most important lessons I learnt during these early years on the wards, and now I make it my goal to treat everyone with respect.

As a midwife, you are required to work in several different settings – in the postnatal ward, the antenatal ward, sometimes in a private maternity unit – but my favourite was the labour ward. I loved everything about it. The unpredictability, the prospect of a new baby, the transition from woman to mother, and the ebb and flow of emotion and excitement. The team would all pull together and work in synchronicity to ensure a safe birth for both the baby and the mum. Maternity services are not perfect, but I felt lucky to work at a hospital where, overall, there was good teamwork and some excellent practitioners.

I will always remember the very first baby I saw being born. I was desperate to work on the labour ward and finally, a few months after I had started as a maternity support worker, I was given the chance. I went and introduced myself to the midwife in charge, and she said the only way to work on the labour ward was to see birth. She took me into a room to assist the midwife, after quickly popping in and asking permission from the patient. A woman was kneeling on the bed, puffing away on the gas and air. My only experience of birth at this point was from watching television. None of my friends had babies yet, and I was the eldest out of all my siblings and cousins, so I really did know very little about babies. It felt incredibly exciting, and I barely knew what to do with myself. As time goes on, you become attuned to the rhythm of labour; the noises that women make, the way they move their body, can tell you a lot. At this point, however, all I knew was that I was about to see something life-changing.

When I entered the room the patient had banished her partner temporarily, as he was irritating her (her exact words can't be repeated). Not too long later, I was sent to retrieve him, and he joined us in supporting her through each wave of contractions. After a few hours, it became clear that she was about to make the transition from pregnant woman to mother. Even with my limited experience of labour, I could tell that birth was imminent. The woman began to bear down and push, and groan in ways that seemed so animalistic and yet natural all at once. Her partner was standing with his head pressed against hers. Before long we were all witnessing their baby daughter being welcomed gently into the world. I felt a wave of emotion bubble up inside me.

There is nothing comparable to watching someone give birth. The atmosphere in the room is always charged, whether with excitement, nerves, fear, adrenaline, or any number of emotions. Women are incredibly powerful and majestic during labour and birth. I was on a high from that experience for at least a couple of weeks. I knew without a doubt that I was going to become a midwife. There was no way I could ever imagine doing anything else. I wanted to be the person who supported another woman as she went through this incredible transformation and made her feel like the absolute Wonder Woman that she is.

Day to day, my work life was mainly cleaning and tidying, although I would assist during more complicated births by fetching instruments or equipment, counting swabs or keeping a record of timings. I loved anything where I could be involved with the patients, even simple things like helping them to the shower. In particular, I loved chatting to the long-stayers on the antenatal ward – women who were unwell, or having very high-risk pregnancies, who might be admitted for weeks or sometimes months – stopping by for a few minutes' chat, or bringing in magazines from home, knowing that even that small interaction might make a huge difference to their day.

One of my guilty pleasures was giving the babies a cuddle. On the postnatal ward, mums and babies are expected to be kept together to encourage bonding. It was frowned upon for us to disrupt that special time by cuddling the babies ourselves. Occasionally mothers would sometimes ask if we could watch their baby while they went to the shower, or an exhausted mother would come to the nurses' station in the middle of the night and ask if we could look after the baby for an hour or two whilst she slept. Some babies didn't want to be put down, so I would eagerly agree to rock or hold the baby during this time. Inspecting their tiny features, wondering who they might become, feeling the warmth and weight of a fresh newborn – it is impossible to hold such a tiny thing without feeling overwhelming emotion. I would sit there and think about my future baby, imagining how it would feel to know that such a tiny person was grown in your body. I was totally in awe of women, and how incredible the female body could be.

At this point in my life, when I was in my early twenties, having my own baby still felt like a lifetime away. Knowing that I would need to train for three years to become a midwife meant that I had put any personal plans on the back burner. I also felt too young to be responsible for an actual human child. The majority of the patients I saw were in their thirties, meaning I always felt far too young to be embarking on a parenthood journey myself. I felt fortunate to already be in a stable relationship with James, so could tick 'Meet man of dreams' off my list. I knew we would marry at some point, and that occupied far more of my headspace than the family I naively assumed would easily follow. I felt no pressure to reproduce, apart from a fascination with midwifery and a desire to experience pregnancy, labour and birth for myself. I was completely taken with the new world that I found myself in.

There were lots of learning opportunities, which I eagerly lapped up as I was desperate to absorb as much as I could. I was fortunate that I was given the opportunity to spend a fortnight in the labour ward theatre, working alongside the scrub team before I could then work in theatre on a regular basis. I learnt the names of all the surgical instruments required for caesarean sections, as well as for other gynaecological surgeries, which I found absolutely fascinating. Most instruments are named after their inventor, and as historically women weren't surgeons, these were almost always men. For example, the Sims' speculum was invented by an American gynaecologist, J. Marion Sims. This type of speculum is used for inspecting inside the vagina or looking at the cervix and commonly used when suturing post-birth.*

---

* Suturing is administering the stitches to repair any damage to the vulva and vagina following childbirth.

The Spencer Wells forceps were invented by an English surgeon, Thomas Spencer Wells, and appear in most suturing packs. I found the history of surgical instruments gruesome and yet compelling too. It felt like I had entered another world, suddenly seeing how certain instruments could be used, and being able to anticipate what the surgeon and scrub team might need. I was slightly intoxicated by the entire process. I often found the hierarchy of hospital life confusing, but in my position at the bottom I felt there was very little I could do about this. I simply carried on, trying to equip myself with as much knowledge as possible.

Occasionally, I had to step outside of my comfort zone. Labour wards tend to be noisy, busy places with lots of action and people rushing around. But unfortunately, more often than we would like, sometimes a room is quiet. Instead of the cry of a baby being born, it's the parents who cry as their baby is born into the world without a sound. Many maternity units have a specific room for bereavement care. These rooms tend to be further away from the hustle and bustle of the main labour ward, although actual services vary between hospitals. Our rooms were numbered, and if there was someone in Room One, we all knew that this meant the loss of a baby. Maternity support workers had no bereavement training at all, and usually weren't involved in the care of these parents, other than making teas and coffees. However, one day the call bell went for Room One, and the midwife was busy looking after someone else. The midwife in charge asked me to answer the bell. I went round to the room and opened the door, not sure what would greet me.

A woman in her late thirties was sitting on the bed, with a cot next to her. Inside, wrapped in a blanket, was a perfectly still baby boy. With dark curly hair, and dark lips, the baby – born at full term – was breathtakingly beautiful. The mother asked me to pass her the baby – that was the reason she'd called. For a moment I was confused. She was not unwell and was perfectly capable of picking up the baby herself. And yet she didn't. She'd called because she felt unable to reach into the cot and lift up her son; her grief was so heavy she couldn't lift anything else.

I looked at the baby, and I am ashamed to admit that I was frightened to pick him up. This was the first time I had ever seen a stillborn baby, and I was wholly unprepared. I remember thinking that it was so vitally important that the mother never saw how terrified I was of holding her baby. I reached into the crib, careful not to touch anything other than the blanket, and picked him up. He was heavy, but without the full weight of a living baby. I gently passed him to his mother.

We talked, and she told me she was single. That this was her only chance at a baby, and it had been taken away. She didn't cry, almost numb to the pain. My knowledge of death at this point was very limited, and even less so around the death of a baby. I told her he was beautiful, and I meant it, but I mostly didn't know what to say and wished I could think of an excuse to leave the room. After passing her the baby, and asking if I could help with anything else, I mumbled an excuse about having tasks to fulfil and left. The room felt suffocating, and I wanted to leave and distract myself.

I came back to the room later on with a cup of tea for the woman, and her family had joined her. They were all looking at the baby, cuddling him, and talking about who he looked like, taking photographs. I remember finding this really confusing at the time, as it felt like they hadn't noticed that the baby was dead. Reflecting back years later, I now know that a baby who has died is still a baby. Someone who was wanted and loved; who looks like other members of the family; who is deserving of love and attention. The family were loving and grieving for a small boy who would not be going home with them.

As a qualified midwife, I have now undertaken bereavement training and I feel equipped to provide better care to grieving families, but as a young MSW I knew nothing of the immense trauma and pain that this woman was going through. As we weren't given large roles in caring for these parents, other than the basic tea-making and observation-taking, I lacked the vital training that could have helped me to understand. Having since lived through my own experience in the very same room, Room One, it is clearer than ever to me that bereavement training is needed for every single person who walks through the doors of the maternity unit for work. Grieving parents will remember what you said, how you said it and how it made them feel. The memories they create over the few hours or days they spend with their baby will last a lifetime. The entire team, from the catering staff all the way to the doctors and midwives, should be taught how to appropriately interact with parents who are living their worst nightmare. Working with both life and death is a privilege. Babies are always beautiful and special, whether they live or die, and it's so important that as midwives we let parents know this.

* * *

After two years as an MSW, I was fortunate to be seconded to train to become a midwife. This meant my hospital trust paid for all the fees associated with my training and continued to pay my salary as well. It is uncommon for training to occur in this way, so I was extremely fortunate. Training takes place at university, but it couldn't have been further from my previous degree experiences. Gone were the days of turning up to seminars with a hangover. We spent 50 per cent of our time in placement, and the other 50 per cent in seminars and lectures, which lasted all day. My course was made up of around a hundred women, and two men. Around a third were straight from school, a third were like me (recent graduates from other courses) and the final third were older, returning to study later in life. In placement, we were supervised by midwives, who taught us the clinical skills we would need. There was a strong nurturing environment from my mentors, who felt like big sisters, and I felt well supported throughout.

I really felt that my time as an MSW had taught me so much about how to talk to patients in a kind and friendly way. I didn't have the same level of skill or knowledge as the midwives, but I used what I did have, which was a smile and some compassion, and I found that this was enough to get by. Now I was a student midwife, I could take these skills and combine them with my new knowledge.

I was always very grateful when a patient allowed a student to help with their care. Without students, there would never be midwives, as we all have to learn our trade somewhere. One of the places that I grew to love working in was the Birth Centre, the low-risk birthing suite in the maternity unit. Women having uncomplicated pregnancies could birth here in a way that encouraged the body's natural birthing process, with minimal intervention from the medical staff. The environment itself was like a spa, and a sense of calm would reach me as I walked into the ward. Each day, going into handover and learning who was giving birth that day, or who had been calling overnight to say they were in early labour, was hugely exciting. Not knowing who was going to walk through the door, and what the situation would be, is enough to keep anyone on their toes.

Midwifery is a very physical job. We use our hands to touch and feel things like a mother's pulse, the position of the baby, the strength of a contraction and so much more. We kneel on the floor next to birthing mothers. We massage, we rub backs, we laugh and cry with our patients. The physical exertion with each shift, and in particular with a birth, leads to an adrenaline rush, and then a subsequent energy crash. Crawling into bed after a long day or night shift, physically aching but knowing I was becoming a smith of a unique craft, would lead to a deep sleep.

A few months into my course, James proposed. We had recently bought a flat and moved to a lovely South-east London suburb. I wish I could say it was a movie-style romantic moment, but in true James-style he was winging it. We had spent an evening out with friends having dinner. On returning, he got down on one knee on our front doorstep and asked me to marry him. We shared our news with our closest friends and family the next morning, and in the afternoon I walked to the shop and bought a wedding magazine. As I was only twenty-five, I was one of the first of my friends to get engaged. I had always dreamed about planning a wedding and finally I was getting my chance! It felt like life was coming together; I was doing the job I loved, in the city I loved, with the man I loved.

I had heard from others that planning a wedding was stressful, but I can honestly say I loved every moment of it. We decided to get married in the summer, so had just over eighteen months to organise the event. I immediately set about deciding on all the details. On my days off from work and study, my mum and I would be busy visiting suppliers, or organising flowers, dresses or stationery. As I was the oldest child among my siblings and cousins, there hadn't been a family wedding on my side in over twenty years. My excitement was through the roof. On quiet night shifts, one of my favourite mentors and I would look at various wedding paraphernalia and talk about our dream nuptials.

Shortly before our wedding, I was due to undertake a placement at a sexual health clinic. Sexual health is an important part of being a midwife, and this placement was one of the most entertaining and interesting parts of my training. This particular clinic was one of the biggest in the UK, and was located in Soho, so there was a strong focus on supporting the LGBTQI+ community based there, along with reducing HIV transmission in the area. The team were incredibly professional, there was a relaxed atmosphere, and all patients and staff were treated with great respect. In other placements I found I was treated as a burden, but here I was greeted with enthusiasm, and all the nurses and doctors I met were keen to teach me their trade.

As a student midwife, I was well versed in female genitalia, but my experiences with the male form were more limited. This was quickly rectified, as the vast majority of people attending the clinic were men. After seeing so many penises with varying infections, lumps and bumps, I was put off my own extracurricular activities for quite some time, much to James' disappointment.

Alongside the huge turnover of people attending for rapid testing for sexually transmitted infections, I was invited to attend a clinic specifically for the trans community. I had never knowingly met any trans people before, but being given the opportunity to chat with the people attending this clinic was a great insight into the needs of those service users in the maternity department. With more trans people entering maternity services than ever before, this sort of exposure is invaluable. I feel fortunate to have trained in London, where the diversity of patients is unlike many other places in the UK. Regardless of the route to parenthood that someone has taken, there is much to learn from every interaction, and nothing is lost by giving compassion. From being an MSW, then going on to become a student midwife, I honed my conversation skills. Being able to strike up a conversation with a complete stranger is an art. My mum always told me that people like talking about themselves as it is what they know and feel confident with, so ask them questions – something she no doubt learnt during her time as a nurse and midwife. Asking questions and appearing interested in someone is a great way to break down barriers and put your patients at ease.

* * *

In July 2016, in front of all our friends and family, James and I married. It was a beautiful, special and emotional day. Not only was I married to a kind and loving man, but it was another item I could tick off the Life Plan. After our wedding, I returned to my placement with a spring in my step, which comes from being a newlywed. Having our own family had begun to enter our thoughts, but, being ever practical, I knew I needed to complete my training first. I couldn't imagine diverting from the Life Plan. My head was telling me that the steps had to be ticked off in the right order. Naively, I was still under the impression that it would be easy for us to have a family, so I felt no pressure at all. I was now twenty-seven, married and living in my own flat in London. We decided that I would complete my final year of midwifery training and then try for our family. I felt in control of my future and assumed that everything would slot into place as it had always seemed to do for me so far.

I was eager to complete my last year of training but felt intimidated by the responsibility of being a qualified midwife, when I would be making my own clinical decisions, which would impact the care and safety of mums and babies. Clinical decision-making is a skill all of its own and takes practice but, most importantly, experience, so as I reached the end of my training, I was given more and more freedom to practise this skill.

One day I was asked to perform a labour assessment on a patient who I had been caring for throughout her pregnancy. The woman was in her mid-thirties and pregnant with her second child, and she had called to say she thought she was in labour but had noticed some bleeding. I greeted her and took her into the assessment room. She seemed in good spirits in between her contractions. I asked to see the bleeding, and was greeted with fresh, sticky, bright-red blood covering the whole pad. Instinctively I was on alert. I quickly continued the rest of my assessment, while checking for any further bleeding. I then explained that I wanted to show the senior midwives the bleeding. In the clinical room, I and three midwives inspected the pad. Was it a heavy show?' Or was it something more sinister? There was not a clear-cut answer, and there was much discussion between us about our thoughts and the potential next steps. The senior midwife, a very experienced practitioner, took the time to ask me what I thought the plan should be. Still being a student midwife and very much erring on the side of caution, I made my recommendation that we should escalate to the labour ward and get a senior review from an obstetrician as quickly as possible. I was terrified both of overreacting to what could potentially be a normal, albeit heavy, show, or missing what could be a potentially life-threatening haemorrhage. Thankfully, the senior midwife agreed and within a few minutes the woman was being reviewed. Fortunately, the labour progressed very quickly, although the bleeding remained heavy throughout, and shortly after a chubby, blond little boy was born with some assistance from a ventouse cup.** I breathed a sigh of relief. Later on, the senior midwife reminded me that even once qualified, you don't have to make decisions by yourself – your colleagues are always there to help and guide you.

I continued to work in various settings: community, labour and birth, antenatal and postnatal wards. I particularly valued the experiences where I got to caseload women. This model of care means the patient sees the same midwife for ideally all her antenatal check-ups; the same midwife attends the birth, and then provides the postnatal care too. This is the gold standard of care; however, sadly it is not very common in the UK. Women will often see a different midwife or health professional at every contact, which can make the care disjointed, and even lead to a lower standard of care, with the potential for things to be missed. It also means there is limited opportunity to build a trusting relationship between mother and midwife. Having a baby can be an overwhelming experience. Being

---

* The show, sometimes known as the mucous plug, is a thick, sticky mucus that blocks up the cervix during pregnancy. Towards the end of pregnancy, or during early labour, this can come away and can sometimes be a little bloody.
** A suction cup, also sometimes known as a kiwi cup, placed on the baby's head. The suction is applied, along with some traction from the doctor, to aid the birth of the baby.

able to ask a professional even the simplest questions, and knowing the answer will be accurate and evidence-based, is priceless.

The year after James and I married, I qualified as a midwife. For my first few shifts, maybe even the first few months, as a qualified midwife, I felt like an imposter. The past five years I had been desperate to wear the teal scrubs that all my midwife colleagues wore, and now it was finally my chance. It felt weird to introduce myself as Sophie the Midwife. I would second-guess my every decision and pester my colleagues for their opinions. Thankfully, it is expected that newly qualified midwives will need lots of support and it was generously given. As time goes on, your confidence builds, but along the way you will make mistakes and hone and perfect the craft of midwifery. Every single intervention or interaction we have with the woman will affect how she feels, how she makes decisions about her care, and potentially the outcome for her and her baby. The first year of being newly qualified is intense and exhausting. Every time a birth deviated from the normal, I would run through in my mind every aspect of the care, and wonder if I could have done something different, which might have led to an alternative outcome. I would cry in the sluice,* and blame myself if a baby was admitted to the neonatal unit, despite it being through no fault of my own. I'd occasionally wake up in the night (or day) thinking about things I had forgotten to do or write down. When I'd call the ward to let one of my colleagues know, I'd often find out that I had done it in the first place. Sometimes I would hear the emergency buzzer going off at home, and jolt into alert mode, ready to respond.

I know I speak for most healthcare professionals when I say we want things to be perfect all the time. Forgiving yourself for not saying the right thing, or for making a mistake, is something you

---

* Sometimes known as the dirty utility room, the sluice is a room on hospital wards where bodily waste products are disposed of.

have to learn to do over time. There are so many aspects of pregnancy, labour and birth that are completely out of everyone's control, and recognising this was a hard but useful lesson. Sometimes births don't go the way the family has planned, and this is always challenging when trying to keep mum and baby safe while also honouring their birth preferences. In the early days, I would worry about whether I'd said or done the right thing. I often struggled with the dictatorial side of obstetrics practice and the fear-mongering, which sometimes goes on. Although this was not a regular occurrence, I occasionally felt women would be persuaded into interventions through fear of putting their baby at risk, rather than being able to make an informed, evidence-based choice. It was difficult to see women reduced to their condition or their room number. 'The lady with GDM [gestational diabetes mellitus] is 1cm dilated' or 'Room Three is having late decels, I think she needs a review' (a late deceleration is where the baby's heart rate drops following a contraction). Part of being a student midwife is learning what sort of midwife you want to be. This includes the language you use, and how you speak about women in your care. Learning how to navigate the complicated NHS maternity services – a system under intense pressure – while also trying to honour each woman and her preferences, is part of the juggling act.

At the same time, James and I began to start talking about the next steps in our personal life. Everything was falling into place. I was married to the man of my dreams, living in a beautiful flat in a leafier part of town and loving my job, and we both felt ready to embark on the next adventure. We had talked about having children together often over the years. We are both family-oriented, and so shortly after I began working as a qualified midwife, we decided that the timing felt right and that we would start trying for a baby. Although at the time I felt pretty confident in my knowledge of pregnancy and birth, it was on my own journey to motherhood that I learnt the most.

3

The Trying Years: Sex, Drugs and Feeling Out of Control

I knew that getting pregnant could take a few months, so I thought that if James and I started early enough, I would still be on track with my Life Plan to have a baby before I was thirty. My mum had brought me into the world aged twenty-eight, and I didn't want to wait too much longer before I became a mother myself. It all fitted in nicely with my checklist and, as always, I assumed that life would give me what I wanted because I had set it out in that way and planned to work hard for it.

True to my schooling and upbringing, I was keen to give myself the best advantage possible so I set about learning all I could on trying to conceive. Due to my midwifery training, I knew more about the female reproductive system than most. I was confident in my understanding of the hormonal changes that happened each month and the principles needed for conception. Having spent years looking after mums and their babies, it didn't even occur to me that it would not be easy to conceive, as I had all this extra knowledge from my career.

Despite my training teaching me that there are only around five fertile days per month, I thought conception was straightforward for the majority, and only more difficult for those women who had left it until much later on. At work I wasn't seeing people in their twenties having IVF, so I naturally assumed that all women in their twenties were incredibly fertile. I had also heard many stories of women in their twenties and thirties who had fallen pregnant by accident, or who had conceived the first month they tried. Almost every time I met someone for their initial midwife appointment, it felt like I heard the same story: they had only stopped their contraception and started 'properly' trying the month before; they weren't expecting it to happen so quickly. Even if that wasn't a true reflection of the stories I was hearing, those were the ones I homed in on. I secretly hoped I might be one of those people. I was young, healthy, active – there seemed no reason why it shouldn't happen for us.

Always pragmatic, I knew it could take up to a year to conceive. The first couple of months were exciting. I would imagine that a fertilised egg was nestling into my womb and feel a warm, fuzzy feeling. We were excited at the possibility that we were heading towards a positive pregnancy test, a family, a bundle of joy of our own. I would imagine my period being a few days late, having to go and buy a pregnancy test, and then seeing those two pink lines. I contemplated how I would tell James and then, after twelve weeks, how we would break the joyous news to our families. I would get butterflies every time I envisioned how perfect everything was going to be. Despite having experience of life with a newborn baby through my job, I chose to only think about the lovely baby cuddles, and to ignore the realities of sleepless nights and sore breasts.

I am not the sort of person to sit and wait patiently. I like to be in control of everything, and I wasn't going to let my body call the shots (oh, the irony!). I downloaded an app to my phone to help me track my ovulation. This involved taking my basal body temperature* each morning and logging it. As you approach ovulation, your temperature

---

* Your lowest resting body temperature – usually taken first thing upon waking in the morning.

drops very slightly, before rising to signal that ovulation has occurred. After a few months a trend tends to appear, indicating the days you may expect ovulation to occur so you can time intercourse appropriately. I dutifully took my temperature before getting out of bed every single morning. The thermometer beeped loudly, much to James' annoyance and to my satisfaction, as it showed that I was putting the requisite effort into conception. I tried my hardest to be consistent, but my night shifts meant I wasn't able to track my ovulation accurately. After six months of trying, and graphs half full of temperatures, I decided to change tactics. A little voice in my head would pipe up and suggest that there was something wrong, that it wasn't going to be easy for us to have a baby. I tried to ignore it – it had only been six months, after all. I knew it could take up to a year and put it down to being oversensitive and a bit controlling. My methodology was wrong, obviously; surely nothing else.

Next, I bought a vaginal thermometer. Yes, you read that right – a thermometer specifically designed for people desperate to conceive, like me. It is a device that you wear in your vagina overnight to track your temperature changes. The result is then uploaded onto an app to work out the average temperature. With no awful beeping to annoy us, this device was a sensor the size of a small egg, which I inserted into my vagina dutifully every night. My attitude to baby-making was one that involved military precision. I must have bypassed the part that was supposed to be fun and carefree. Instead, I wanted our baby to come as quickly as possible and was therefore going to try my hardest to make that happen. The vaginal thermometer gave a more accurate reading, but the problem of night shifts still persisted. Our body's natural circadian rhythm does not expect you to be awake at night and asleep during the day, so despite my best efforts this still wasn't the best method for me to track ovulation. The key to temperature checking is consistency, and my ever-changing shift patterns were anything but consistent.

This led to me moving on to ovulation sticks. I peed on a stick every day to wait for a surge in my luteinising hormone, which would indicate ovulation was approaching. I would tape all the sticks to a piece of paper, in order to clearly see when the line had reached it darkest, therefore highlighting that I could expect ovulation usually around twenty-four hours later. I would analyse the sticks daily, sometimes multiple times a day, to see which line was darker. I would look at photos on the internet of other people's ovulation sticks for comparison. I would send photos of ovulation sticks to trusted friends for their opinion on the shade of each line and the portent they held. It became a lot more obvious when ovulation was happening than when I was tracking my temperature and seemed to solve the problem of the inconsistent shift patterns I was working. The new issue was that both James and I were often on diametrically opposite shifts ourselves. If I was on nights, he would be on day shifts at his pub, and vice versa. It felt like we were keeping the bed warm for each other, but never managing to sleep in it at the same time. Some months we would miss the window of opportunity because one or both of us were working, and I would weep knowing that another month was passing us by.

I would chat to James about the various bits of information I had gleaned. To me it was all fascinating, but I'm sure it became slightly tedious to hear in exact detail how an egg was released from an ovary. James humoured me and would feign interest. Every time I introduced something into our routine that was supposed to result in our baby, he simply nodded and complied. I suspect he could sense that even after less than a year of trying, my desperation and despair was growing. I had spoken to one or two friends, but on the whole I kept our baby-making escapades to ourselves. I was still hoping we would be able to share our happy news before too long. The one or two friends I did confide in then went on to conceive very quickly, and although I was happy for them, I felt a deep sadness for myself.

I began to gather and read anything and everything I could find on fertility and baby-making. I started what we now jokingly call the infertility library. I bought book after book after book that each explained the 'best' methods to help conception. Some books were medical, some were memoirs and some were written by alternative therapy practitioners. One topic that came up over and over again was cervical mucus, a subject that even as a midwife I knew very little about. Throughout the menstrual cycle mucus is released from your cervix. In the different stages of the cycle, the mucus changes in consistency. As ovulation approaches it begins to look like egg whites. Various books explained that the presence of egg-white cervical mucus was a fantastic way of predicting ovulation, and that this mucus was essential in aiding the sperm to find their way up to the cervix and into the uterus. I am well versed in bodily fluids, thanks to midwifery, but this mucus was very alien to me. Much as I tried and tried to understand it, I just couldn't differentiate when it looked like egg whites in consistency. I would rub and stretch the mucus, and compare it to descriptions in various fertility textbooks, but nothing that was coming out of my vagina looked remotely like egg whites. I was sure that no one else I knew was going to such lengths to have a baby. I wasn't even sure any of my friends or colleagues would know what cervical mucus was, so I didn't dare bring it up.

Talk of babies was always rife at work. Having such a large number of women working together, it seems like midwives are pregnant constantly. No one at work ever mentioned not being able to conceive. The majority of the midwives I worked with were a similar age to me, in either their twenties or early thirties, and seemed to pop out babies as soon as they got married. On shift, conversations around whether we would have an epidural, an induction, a sweep were all commonplace. It was so casual, like talking about the weather. As the months went on, and my own baby-making efforts seemed not to be coming to fruition, I would find these conversations more and more painful. In addition, patients would often ask whether I had children.

Unsurprisingly, James and I had lots of sex. We tried having sex every day. We tried having sex every other day. We tried having sex on certain days of the cycle. We tried having sex in the mornings. We tried having sex in the evenings. We tried having sex in 'better' positions. We tried sperm-friendly lubricant. We tried a vaginal cup to keep the semen in after sex. Each new activity seemed more ridiculous and less enjoyable than the last. However, I was willing to give anything a chance, in the hope that this might be the last month of trying. James and I would make jokes out of the various lengths we were going to, but they never seemed that funny. We both tried to carry on and pretend that it was all normal, that it would work itself out in the end.

One thing that soon became obvious was that relentlessly trying for a baby rapidly loses its shine. When my period showed up month after month after month, the task of trying became more laborious. Not only were our shift patterns incompatible and uncooperative, but despite desperately wanting a baby, after several months I was not interested in sex at all, other than for the purpose of procreation. There was no pleasure involved at all for me. I started to think that perhaps my body wasn't playing ball. It didn't occur to me that the problem might lie with James; I assumed our lack of success was all my fault. This in turn led to my self-confidence taking a nosedive. I didn't feel attractive, I didn't want to have sex, but I wanted a baby, so I persevered.

I was driven to have sex in the first two weeks of the cycle, knowing that this was THE time for conception. Then, once ovulation had been confirmed, we wouldn't go near each other for the next two weeks, each needing some breathing space before repeating the process over again the next month. So the cycle continued: neither of us enjoying having sex, but each feeling obliged to give it a chance in case this would be the month. The long-term goal, the end result, was our family – more important than any short-term unhappiness or struggle.

One morning I was returning from a night shift just as James was about to get up to go to work. I was about to get into bed with another night shift on the horizon but, having been informed by my ovulation sticks that it was 'go time', I demanded that James and I have sex right away. I was tired, sweaty and absolutely determined that we were not going to miss the opportunity this month. James wearily agreed, despite having got home from work in the small hours of the morning and being up first thing to open his pub again. Needless to say, our venture was not very successful. The pressure on James to perform when his tired and hormonal wife was demanding sex was not a recipe for romance. I sank into a deep sad sleep afterwards, before waking that evening and returning to work. Another month without a baby. At work, I pretended I felt fine, while cuddling each newborn in the hospital a little more tightly, wondering if I would ever have my own.

Dr Google became my best friend as I searched out ways I could aid conception. I began to feel like a woman obsessed. There was not a single moment in the day when I wouldn't be thinking about having a baby. I hate to play into stereotypes of desperate, broody women, but honestly there was little space in my brain for anything else. The harder it seemed to be, the more desperately I wanted it. I couldn't believe it was so difficult to have a baby. Being surrounded by bumps and babies only highlighted the emptiness that I felt in my own womb. I joined blogs and forums to hear what other women were saying. I read pages and pages of posts to see if there were any tips that other women tried that might help us. I bought and read more books for my infertility library. I began to try all sorts of alternative ideas – it didn't matter how outlandish it seemed; I was willing to try it in the hope that it might bring us our longed-for baby.

I overhauled our diet. We have always enjoyed food and cook most things from scratch. But I took this to a new level. I cut out sugar completely from my diet, including most fruits (I had read sugar was an endocrine disruptor and not good for egg quality). Simple foods such as bananas became like poison to me, as they have a high sugar content. I would allow myself only one portion of fruit a day, and it had to be something low in sugar and high in antioxidants, like berries. I loaded up on vegetables and restricted my carbohydrates. Colleagues would comment that I would never indulge in any of the various chocolates that were gifted to us by kind patients. I would brush it off and pretend I was on a diet. One day I read an article about peas making you infertile and cried. How could so many of my patients get pregnant with such ease, and here I was debating whether to cut out peas from my already restricted diet? This was where I drew the line.

I bought cookbooks aimed at helping conception through diet, then would recreate the recipes to varying degrees of success. I stocked the cupboard and fridges with sperm- and egg-friendly foods – mainly organic vegetables and whole grains. I boiled up leftover chicken carcasses and bones to make bone broth, said to be good for fertility. I would hide superfood powders in my cooking and feed it to James to try to keep him in tip-top shape, too. I bought fertility tea, which I drank twice a day. It tasted absolutely vile, but I dutifully swallowed it down morning and evening in the hope a baby would shortly follow.

I began to make my own fertility drink, which consisted of a whole lemon, some ginger, walnut oil and various powdered supplements all blended into one. I would only drink this out of a metal straw, as I was concerned it would erode my teeth due to all the acid. I would drink two litres of this every single day without fail, as I had read somewhere on the internet that someone had drunk this and miraculously conceived a baby. Despite knowing that I hadn't come across any patients who had mentioned any of my fertility hacks, I still hoped that one would work for me. Deep down I knew I was clutching at (metal) straws, but I couldn't bear the thought of not trying these things in case they were the answer. My self-esteem was at an all-time low, and every waking thought was about ways I could improve our chances of conceiving a baby.

As I scoured the internet trying to find things that could help me, any of the rigour and attention to evidence-based practice that I used when working went out of the window. At home I was a woman on a mission. As the months passed by, I became desperate for professional help but knew I would be dismissed by my GP if we hadn't been trying for a year, and at this point only eight months had passed. What shocked me was how quickly my desperation had grown. I hadn't expected to become so obsessed so quickly. I began to count down the weeks until we could make an appointment and seek external help. I think there were genuinely very few things that I wouldn't have considered trying at this time in my life.

I would frame all my endeavours as self-care. I was looking after my body and ensuring I was in the best condition to grow a baby. I believed that if I worked hard enough, I would be rewarded. I wasn't sure why it was taking so long, but I was certain that the more effort I put in, eventually it would pay off. I bought fertility crystals. I tried tapping, reiki, acupuncture, even seed cycling, where you eat certain seeds at different times of your menstrual cycle. I told myself that it was all in my best interests and that I was simply looking after myself. Looking back, I can see how unhealthy some of my habits were. I had become so fastidious about my diet that I found it hard to eat out and increasingly difficult to socialise, as I felt even one naughty meal might derail my chances of becoming a mother. I could no longer walk into a shop and buy simple products like shampoo. I would have to look up the ingredients and work out if I considered it fertility-friendly.

Then I moved on to supplements. Not content with the recommended folic acid and vitamin D, I spent hundreds (maybe even close to thousands) of pounds on vitamins and supplements, all aimed at improving egg quality. I would swallow between ten and twenty pills throughout the day, all with my ovaries in mind. There was also a military precision to the timings of these vitamins. I would take a small pill box around with me if I wasn't at home, rattling as I walked, containing the various tablets I would take throughout the day. I never missed a single dose, so ingrained was this behaviour in my daily activities. Each supplement was carefully researched, and I only bought premium brands, all with a premium price tag. I bought supplements for James, too, and insisted he took them every day. He obliged, mainly because he didn't have the energy to argue with me. Ever the optimist, he was hopeful that we would still be able to build our family without any outside intervention. I suspect he was shocked by the intensity of my dedication to Project Baby. Over the years I have been half terrified of the effects of my self-medicating, but also terrified that if I didn't keep on taking them, I might miss my opportunity for a baby.

And then came the wheatgrass. Possibly the most disgusting of all the things I tried in the pursuit of motherhood. In a search-engine rabbit hole, I found many women proclaiming the health benefits of wheatgrass. I bought an organic green powder from a health shop, and it tasted like mud. I would mix this into smoothies to mask the taste. Then, after further research, it appeared that whole wheatgrass, rather than powdered, was the most effective, so I bought some extortionately expensive frozen wheatgrass. Each morning I would drink a shot of the vile green liquid. It would often make me heave, and I would chase it down with something else to rid my mouth of the taste. Then, in a final bid to cajole my ovaries into action, I began to grow wheatgrass in my kitchen. Following online videos, I bought the seeds and grew trays of grass. Once tall enough, I would blend it with a small amount of water and drink the mixture each morning. Surprisingly, this tasted the best out of all my wheatgrass experiments. After months of this routine, I finally decided that enough was enough. I didn't want to start my day drinking something that made me retch. I still have about five bags of wheatgrass seeds in my shed, but I'm thinking about using it to seed my lawn, as I could never bring myself to drink it again.

Following the supplement overhaul, I began an assault on the contents of our house. Firstly, I threw out every single piece of plastic that we had in our kitchen. I'd read somewhere on Dr Google that chemicals in plastic could be endocrine disruptors, and this could be the reason we hadn't conceived. James came home one day to find that I had replaced all our Tupperware with glass and taken the plastic offenders to the local charity shop. Bemused, he didn't say anything. I was prone to outbursts of tears or rage in my frustration at the lack of progress in making a baby. He simply carried on and agreed that glass was probably better for the environment. I preached to friends about how we were becoming greener but was careful never to expose the real reason behind it all. Admitting there was a problem to other people felt like admitting I was failing.

Next, I attacked our bathroom cupboards, giving the entire contents to my sister after explaining that James and I were trying to be healthier and more responsible towards the environment. I replaced everything with only natural products, which would apparently be kinder to my eggs and my ovaries. New shampoo, shower gel, conditioner, make-up, facial products, moisturiser, deodorant, even toothbrushes and toothpaste; the whole lot was replaced. I would spend vast amounts of time researching each product and finding an alternative that was non-toxic. While I felt a complete lack of control in terms of making a baby, these small steps helped me to feel that I was doing something positive. My thinking was that each small change had the potential to increase my fertility marginally, and that all these small gains would eventually equate to a baby.

It didn't make sense that I was working so hard, but still my period showed up month after month. After being taught that working hard meant you could achieve your goals, I was beginning to feel short-changed. I also began to feel more and more out of control. My life had been going to plan; everything had happened how I had wanted it to, and now I was stuck.

* * *

I didn't tell many people that we were struggling to conceive; instead, I pretended that we hadn't been trying very long, and that I wasn't worried. I tried to seem relaxed about the situation, while on the inside I was growing increasingly frustrated with well-meaning friends and family telling us that we would be next. I told James I was concerned that something serious was amiss. He convinced me to wait until our twelve months was up before we saw our GP, still hopeful that it might happen naturally. I began slyly to ask pregnant friends questions to see if they had any tips. A close friend told me not to get up after sex, and to put a pillow under my bottom. She had been trying for a baby for a few months, and the first month she'd done this, she had conceived her child. I felt a bit patronised that she assumed I hadn't already tried this – I had. Knowing that this had not previously made any difference, but not wanting to miss out, I dutifully obliged again. Not only was it uncomfortable and undignified, but I couldn't help laughing at the ridiculousness of it all. Spoiler alert: it didn't work.

At the hospital, I would hear women say how they weren't trying to get pregnant or how they got pregnant on the first month of trying, and I would stare at them in disbelief. Why was this so hard for us? What was I doing wrong? I even began to question my understanding of basic anatomy. Were we having sex wrong? I couldn't work out why we hadn't even had a late period, let alone a positive pregnancy test. I felt increasingly alone. The hospital in London where I worked cared for a high proportion of mothers aged thirty-five and over, and many women in their forties. It was rare that I would encounter a patient in their early twenties, let alone a teenager. At this time, I was in my late twenties, and so the majority of the women I was interacting with at work were roughly ten years older than me. I just wasn't seeing women of my age struggling with fertility issues, so I felt a deep sense of loneliness and alienation from other women. Admittedly the demographic at my place of work was skewed, but I didn't know any different, having never worked anywhere else. Here I was trying my hardest, and yet women who were ten to fifteen years older than me were managing it with ease. It was a difficult time, and I began to question whether there was something very wrong with me, and whether I would ever hold my own baby in my arms.

* * *

When my period showed up as reliably as ever each month, I saw it as my own personal failure and began to question whether I was worthy of motherhood after all. After nine months had passed, I felt I was at breaking point. Friends and family had fallen pregnant without even thinking about it, and we were no closer. Despite knowing that it could take a year to conceive, I wasn't sure I could face waiting a further three months until we could get help. There was a cycle of hope and grief with each month that passed. In those nine months since we had excitedly decided that the timing felt right to expand our family, I had changed from a happy, carefree twenty-something into a shadow of my former self. I called up my GP and made an appointment for a couple of weeks' time.

As all my efforts felt like they were in vain, I felt ready to hand over the reins to the medical professionals. After all, I worked in healthcare and had huge faith in all things science. I had tried to cajole my body into cooperating by any means possible. Now I was ready for the big guns: the doctors. One thing I know I can look back and say is that I tried my absolute hardest, but I was willing to admit defeat. Trying for a baby really was a trying process.

4

Unwomanhood

Bodies are amazing things. They carry out all sorts of complex processes without us even having to think about or acknowledge them. Breathing, digestion, gas exchange and so much more. When an organ or body part doesn't work as we expect, we are fortunate to have modern medicine to help us fix it. In the UK, thanks to our wonderful NHS, we are even more fortunate that a trip to the doctor or the hospital is free at the point of delivery. A visit to the doctor and some treatment will hopefully put your body on the path to recovery.

Unless that dysfunctional organ is your uterus. Infertility is not just seen as an organ gone wrong; there are complex social connotations. In some ways, it feels as though it is a reflection of you as a person. If a kidney stops working, there is no question of whether you are deserving of treatment for your condition. We accept that if there is something wrong with an organ, we should attempt to fix it. However, if that organ is your womb or ovaries, complete strangers can and will pass judgement on your ability to be a parent, simply because a part of your body is not working correctly. It is somehow seen as 'meant to be' that way. Not a problem that could be fixed, but instead a reflection of your ability to nurture and love a genetic child.

I have heard unkind comments which have suggested that those requiring fertility treatments are 'not meant to be a parent'. Not only is this an incredibly cruel comment, but it has absolutely no basis in truth. In reality, there is no such thing as being 'meant' or 'not meant' to be a parent. For the most part, people are free to choose whether they become parents or not. For those of us who need some help to become parents, there are numerous ways to get there, all of which are completely valid. Becoming a parent through other means, such as fertility treatment, surrogacy or adoption, does not mean that you are any less a parent than those who conceived and birthed their children themselves.

There is a huge stigma surrounding people who are not able to reproduce. As the vast majority of people have children, if you are unable to join this shared experience, you are seen as an outsider. On a basic level, reproduction is key to the survival of any species. The stigma of infertility is even greater if you belong to a Black, Asian or minority ethnic (BAME) group. As a white middle-class woman, I am not in the best position to comment on the specifics of living with infertility as a Black or Asian person; however, the statistics speak for themselves. Those from BAME backgrounds are older when they do finally receive fertility treatments, and these treatments have much lower success rates.* Whether this is because BAME people delay seeking treatment due to stigma within their communities, or because there is unconscious (or indeed conscious) bias across society that makes it harder for them to access care, more needs to be done to understand why these inequalities exist and how we can challenge and change them.

The fear of social consequences when admitting to infertility and assisted reproductive treatments are deep rooted. I know of one

---

* For more information on the fertility statistics for ethnic minority patients, see the Human Fertilisation & Embryology Authority website: https://www.hfea.gov.uk/about-us/news-and-press-releases/2021-news-and-press-releases/fertility-treatment-less-successful-for-ethnic-minority-patients-new-figures-reveal/

patient, Trudy, who needed IVF to conceive her little girl. At the birth she haemorrhaged and ended up critically unwell in the high-dependency unit. Once she'd recovered, an unhelpful visitor to her home commented that perhaps her traumatic delivery was in fact proof that she was not meant to be a mother after all. Nature had tried to tell her something when she couldn't conceive, and she had gone against this with fertility treatment. I was gobsmacked when Trudy recounted this to me. After all she had gone through, and then being so unwell, her guest had no consideration for the emotional ripples these comments could cause. I reassured Trudy that I felt she was destined for motherhood, and that all she had endured was a testament to the love she had for her daughter.

Sometimes women internalise the rhetoric they are hearing, and then begin to tell themselves a similar narrative: your body does not want you to have a child. That must mean you are not worthy of a child. Clearly there is no link between the functionality of your body parts and your parenting ability. The possibility that you might not be able to conceive, carry and birth a child without assistance is something that most people never have to think about, as only around 10 to 15 per cent of couples will experience fertility issues.

Becoming pregnant can seem so simple in theory. You decide to have a baby, have unprotected sex, and then nine months later the child is in your arms. I knew almost nothing about infertility, and as far as I was aware, until we started trying to conceive, I was fertile. I had my periods every month, and I was young and healthy. I didn't smoke, didn't really drink and ate a healthy balanced diet. During my midwifery training, we covered very little about fertility treatments. I'm not sure we had a single session about it, despite tens of thousands of babies being conceived this way every year. Midwifery is the profession of pregnancy, so you would think infertility at the very least would be covered in the teaching.

During my second year of training, we were required to spend time working outside of maternity but in related areas, such as the neonatal intensive care unit (NICU), the main theatres and also the gynaecology department. On one such day, I was shadowing a senior nurse who ran a menopause clinic. She would see patients who were struggling with menopause symptoms, and in some cases would counsel them on hormone replacement therapy (HRT), or other lifestyle changes they could make to ease their symptoms. I knew next to nothing about menopause and found this nurse to be so incredibly knowledgeable; it was inspiring to listen to her.

One woman who walked through the doors that day was Julie, who appeared much younger than the rest of the visitors we'd seen. She was aged forty-four, but her appearance was much younger, like someone in their late thirties. She sat down and placed a huge folder full of papers on the desk, mostly previous hospital notes. Unlike the other patients, Julie was not there to discuss how she could manage her menopause symptoms. She was there to discuss how she could have a baby. I was a little confused at first, unsure if it was normal to be discussing this in a menopause clinic. Julie, who was well equipped with pages of blood results, scan results and IVF treatment protocols she had already tried, began discussing the various options she had for regulating some of her hormone levels.

I had absolutely no idea what any of the blood results meant, or whether Julie did have a chance at conceiving a child. When I look back, my immediate thoughts were pretty judgemental. Didn't Julie realise she was too old to have a child? I was in my mid-twenties at this point, with no idea of the journey that I would be embarking on in a few years. I couldn't understand why Julie didn't accept that she had missed her chance. It seemed plain to me, looking at it from a medical perspective (albeit a very junior one), that the odds were not in her favour. Her body had already started the transition away from fertility and into perimenopause, and yet her heart still yearned to hold a little baby in her arms. I knew nothing of the overwhelming sense of desperation and urgency that longing for a child brought.

I made a judgement based solely on her age, giving no thought to the emotional upheaval and journey that Julie might have undergone so far. I had no notion at the time of the extreme lengths women are often prepared to go to in order to have a child. That for some women, and I now consider myself one of them, it is impossible to give up on that dream of having your own child. I'll never know whether this woman ever got to hold her much-longed-for baby, but I do often think that if I was in the same position, I would be fighting with every ounce of my being.

Years later, learning that my body was not going to make a baby without assistance was one of the hardest pills I've ever had to swallow. The longer we tried for a baby, the more miserable I became. Before we had any investigations into the cause of our infertility, I assumed that the blame lay solely with me. I was quick to take on the responsibility, and also the emotional burden of trying and failing to have a baby. It was my body that wasn't getting pregnant every month, so in my mind it was all my fault.

Historically, infertility was always seen as a female issue. Take Henry VIII, who famously had six wives, moving swiftly between them in the search for a male heir. At the time it was seen as the fault of each of his wives that no male heir could be produced, with no evidence to prove this. It couldn't possibly be the fault of a man – and especially not a king – that many of his wives were unable to carry a child to term. Nowadays it is known that there is roughly an equal split in the causes of infertility, with 30 per cent of issues attributed to females, 30 per cent to males and 30 per cent due to both partners or unexplained causes.[*] Even with these statistics, nearly all the tests and investigations focus on the female, with only basic non-invasive tests being performed on the male partner. I was quick to assume that our

---

[*] See the British Fertility Society website: https://www.britishfertilitysociety.org.uk/fei/what-is-infertility/

inability to conceive was caused by me, which did in fact turn out to be correct, but I had no reason to jump to this conclusion other than social conditioning.

I internalised a narrative that told me I was less worthy because I couldn't conceive, and I began to chip away at my own self-esteem. How could I expect my husband to love me? To find me attractive? To not seek solace in the arms of a more fertile woman? I began to question whether our relationship could stand this test. I assumed that I was destined to be alone, while James could find another woman to build a family with. There was nothing to suggest that James actually thought any of these things, but in my mind it was a foregone conclusion. I saw myself turning into all the stereotypes I could think of. Haggard, wrinkled, bitter and alone.

If the situation had been reversed, and the problem had lay with James, not for one second would I have portioned any blame on him. I would have accepted that conception would be difficult for us, but I would have faced the problem head on with him. I couldn't allow myself this same compassion; I saw myself as defective and unfeminine. On more than one occasion I asked James if he was planning on leaving me if we never had a child together. His unwavering support and belief in our ability to live fulfilling lives with or without children has often kept me going. He has always insisted that it is OUR infertility, not just mine. He has always been clear that he wants a baby with me, so leaving me for another woman wouldn't solve the problem. Despite his kind words, I found it difficult to believe him and assumed that after long enough he would get bored of being childless and move on to a younger woman, whose ovaries worked.

At the time I found it difficult to explain, but now I realise I began to doubt myself as a woman. I wasn't sure how I fitted into what felt like a world where most people were able to conceive easily. I had always assumed I would become a mother. It wasn't something I had ever questioned, as it seemed so obvious that it was in my destiny. After we tried and tried for a baby, I began to wonder whether this would ever happen for us. Was I destined to be a childless woman?

I couldn't imagine a life without children. Ideally, I wanted three. Would I have to rethink my whole life? What would a life without children look like? I am fully aware that many women choose not to have children, or are unable to have children, and go on to have completely fulfilling lives. Sadly, it was difficult for me to imagine myself in that scenario. I became stuck in a spiral of feeling inadequate compared to other women. At work I would see people in their most fertile and blooming state and feel empty and hollow.

I decided that if I could not be a mother (however that came to fruition), I would have to leave midwifery. At my lowest points, I could no longer bear to be Sophie the Midwife knowing that I would never be Sophie the Mother. I adored my midwifery career, but I decided that if I reached forty-three and there was no one to call me 'Mummy', I would turn my life upside down. Running away to the Caribbean or finding a childless commune somewhere both sounded like appealing solutions. Forty-three was a completely arbitrary age that I plucked from nowhere. I couldn't imagine being on this fertility rollercoaster for nearly fifteen years, but at the same time I wanted to know I had exhausted every option before giving up. I knew I couldn't live through my own heartbreak every time I saw a woman becoming a mother, knowing that I might never get to experience that for myself.

My brain spent months being permanently on overdrive. It would race from one situation to another. Before having ever even stepped inside an IVF clinic, I was researching every option that was available to us. Would we consider donor eggs, surrogacy, adoption? My answer was yes to all of the above. I simply could not imagine my life without a child. My sense of self was hinged on becoming a mother, whatever that looked like. I could not see a place for me in a society where the woman as mother is put on a pedestal, and the barren woman is pitied and feared.

How do you define womanhood and motherhood? Although they are separate, I felt that on some level these two states were intrinsically linked: motherhood is seen as virtuous and selfless, and the message I had absorbed was that becoming a mother was the ultimate feminine act. There is a huge amount of reverence for mothers, and rightly so, as they do a thankless, difficult and often under-appreciated job. Throughout my childhood, Mother's Day was a day to celebrate and thank my own mother for all she did for us, but once we had started trying for a baby, Mother's Day became torturous. Social media would show photos of handmade cards and breakfast in bed, and on the ward we would celebrate the amazing work the mums did. It would always be a special moment if a baby was born on Mother's Day. I used to enjoy those moments, but they would be bittersweet. Would I ever be able to celebrate in the same way?

I found myself withdrawing from friends who conceived easily and had straightforward pregnancies. I would dread seeing couples who were newly married, as I would always be anticipating a pregnancy announcement. I was well practised at putting my game face on and uttering the necessary congratulations. Then, once I was in a safe place, I would often break down in tears at the seeming unfairness of it all. Having always worked with women, suddenly I felt as though I was on the outside looking in. I was excluded from the Mum Club. In my mind, that made me less of a woman.

I did know several midwives who had not gone on to become mothers. I had never questioned why, but now I wondered if it was through choice or circumstance. One particular midwife, Jodie, was in her late forties when I first met her. Jodie was open about the fact that she wanted to be a mother, but she had never found the right man to settle down with. Instead, she threw all her efforts into mothering her patients and the other midwives. She was the type of midwife that you would be happy to have on the same shift as you. She had a wicked sense of humour, wasn't afraid of anyone and would stand up for what she believed was right. She gave me the confidence to look after complex cases. She sat with me and helped me suture post-birth when I was newly qualified. She put a smile on my face after she found me crying in the sluice after a difficult shift. She would be the midwife to come into your room if your patient was struggling during the last moments of birth. She had such a way of mothering the patients and always knew the right thing to say to get them through the final push (pun intended). After many, many years on the labour ward, she eventually left to travel the world. A loss to midwifery, but I think of her often and all she taught me, so her legacy lives on.

Meanwhile, my body seemed to punish me with the worst parts of womanhood, but with none of the benefits of fertility. My periods arrived, red and angry every month. My face was also red and angry with hormonal spotty outbreaks. The cyclical nature of the female reproductive system made it seem like groundhog month. Each month revolved around thoroughly inspecting my body but having no idea of the secrets that were being kept deep within. It seemed ironic that as a midwife I had insider knowledge of the inner workings of the female body, but my own body seemed a complete mystery to me.

Not only did infertility confuse my sense of womanhood, it also challenged my view of my body as something that was fully functioning. My infertility did not impede my day-to-day living – from the outside you could not see that I was infertile – and yet, one of the most basic biological processes in my body did not work. In reality, fertility treatment doesn't actually fix the problem of infertility. It can give you a baby, but the problems still remain. You can have children and still remain infertile. The entire fertility treatment industry is aimed at giving couples a baby, but it does very little to allow them to conceive naturally and rectify whatever the issue is.

And yet I had such overwhelming confidence in the female body at work. During pregnancy, the most incredible changes happen to a woman's body. She takes two cells, an egg and a sperm, and can create a whole new human being in less than a year. The shifts and accommodations that occur within the body to support this life are phenomenal. One of my all-time favourite parts of midwifery is palpating a baby within its mother's abdomen – when you feel which position the baby is lying in, and the baby wriggles and kicks beneath your hands. I am constantly in awe of the body's amazing feat, which appears so easy.

During labour and birth, women are powerhouses. The body goes through a remarkable transformation, without any thought required. The body knows exactly how to birth a baby. And yet my own body was not capable of doing a single remarkable thing. At work I would be championing and cheering on women, telling them how amazing they were and reminding them of all their body was capable of. At home, I was confused, disappointed and angry that my own body held no such power. I felt weak and unremarkable, empty and alone.

Living with infertility requires you to grieve the life you thought you would live. You must say goodbye to the ideas you once held of making a baby through a loving act with your partner. My freedom to choose whether or not I became a mother was removed from me. Instead, it was put down to science and luck. And yet I have seen unkind comments online along the lines that infertile people should stop complaining as there are much bigger problems in the world. I agree that I live a privileged life with much to be thankful for. But not being able to have a baby isn't as simple as wanting a new pair of shoes, and them being out of stock everywhere. Wanting a baby involves longing for a whole plethora of experiences and being unable to reach them. The positive pregnancy test, the announcement, the pregnancy itself where you can feel a small person wriggling around inside of you. Watching your body change shape as it accommodates the new little person, decorating the nursery, attending antenatal classes, packing the hospital bag – and as a midwife I had always wanted to live through the experience of labour. I felt no fear of labour, only awe and excitement. I wanted to have skin-to-skin contact with my tiny baby, to feel their warmth, to breastfeed them, to know that only I could soothe their crying. All these experiences, which I saw as written in my future, were suddenly hanging in the balance.

At some points I felt so low I wasn't sure I would be able to carry on living if there were no children in my life. I know how dramatic that sounds, but infertility chips away at your self-esteem and sense of self-worth. I felt that James or my family would be better off without me. I thought I was a burden, and that my sadness was too much for other people to bear. I felt miserable, and assumed other people saw me as sad and unhappy or someone to be pitied. Although James and I told few people about our infertility, I imagined us being gossiped about. I assumed other people questioned why we had been married so long without having a child. I lost the ability to find joy in day-to-day activities. I began to live my life for the sole purpose of having a child. I was lost.

5

Navigating the System

As midwives are taught very little about IVF and the process surrounding it, I remember more than one occasion as a newly qualified midwife when patients who were pregnant following IVF would mention medication they were taking and I had absolutely no idea what it was or what it was used for. So I was very much in the dark when it came to navigating the system myself.

While waiting for my GP appointment, I felt both excited and terrified. I was hopeful that someone might be able to help us or tell us how to fix the issue. At the same time it was hugely scary having to admit out loud that things weren't working as they should, and equally frightening to think that perhaps nothing could be done. I also hoped I would be one of those people I had heard of in casual conversations who were having all their fertility investigations and then just happened to fall pregnant naturally.

On the day of my appointment, in between shifts I walked the few roads to our local practice and sat in the waiting room staring at the book I had brought with me, not taking in a single word. When my name appeared on the screen, I walked into the consulting room and saw a young female GP, probably in her early thirties. She asked what had brought me to her room that day. Despite having played this scenario over in my head again and again, I didn't seem able to make the words leave my mouth.

Eventually I explained that my husband and I had been trying for a baby, and it wasn't happening for us. The tension that had been bubbling up in my chest for nearly a year seemed to spill out of me. I burst into tears – big, heavy sobs that were moving my chest. The GP was kind and said that they could run some tests. She also added that I was much younger than her, and she hadn't had a baby yet, and that I had plenty of time. I'm sure she thought this was supposed to comfort me. It did the opposite. I felt even worse for being so young and supposedly fertile, and still failing to make a baby.

One of my biggest bugbears is the assumption that young people don't need fertility treatment. That IVF is only for women in their forties, or even that IVF will work if you are young. None of these things are guaranteed. Of course, the age of your eggs is important, and statistically the younger you are, the more likely you are to conceive either spontaneously or via assisted reproductive technologies. That said, plenty of people in their twenties and early thirties need help to have a baby. Whatever the woman's age or circumstances, IVF success rates are really quite low – approximately 30 per cent of cycles in women under thirty-five are successful, and it's an even lower percentage if you are older – so there's only a small chance of success if you end up on this route.[*]

Back then, I knew none of these facts or figures. All I knew was that I desperately wanted to have a baby, and it looked like we would need some help. I left the surgery clutching a blood request form, with instructions to have certain blood tests on exact days of my cycle. Eyes wet with crying, I walked home feeling nervous about what might be in store for us, but anxious to get moving towards my

---

[*] For more on the statistics of IVF, see the Human Fertilisation & Embryology Authority website: https://www.hfea.gov.uk/about-us/publications/research-and-data/fertility-treatment-2019-trends-and-figures/

goal of bringing a baby home.

Being able to attend the local hospital for my blood tests on those specific days proved trickier than I thought due to my shift work. I needed to have my follicle stimulating hormone (FSH) checked on day three of my cycle, and my progesterone checked on day twenty-one.* Eventually I managed to get them both checked, and so began the first of many (many) anxious waits to hear back from my GP.

In the meantime, I busied myself with work. It was a particularly hectic time in the maternity department. One night on my way home from a shift in the Birth Centre, I cried on the train. I had looked after a lovely couple that I had seen a few times throughout their pregnancy. They were a young American couple, who had come over from Canada as Michael, the husband, had a job as a diplomat. It was their first baby, and they were hoping for a pool birth. They had been in the night before, and I had assessed Bree and found that she was in the early stages of labour. I advised that she went home and tried to rest as much as possible while waiting for her labour to establish. The following night she came back in with strong, long contractions. She was graceful and composed throughout her labour, and the connection between her and her husband was incredible to witness. They were one team, with Michael supporting Bree through every contraction both physically and emotionally. After several hours, Bree and Michael's baby entered the world via a calm and peaceful pool birth. It was so beautiful, and I feel so lucky to have been part of it. Yet part of me was jealous. I wanted to experience that. I wanted James to rub my back and tie up my hair. I wanted him to offer me sips of water in between contractions. I wanted the whole lot, and it felt so very far from my grasp.

It was becoming increasingly difficult not to be affected by my

---

* Follicle stimulating hormone is the hormone in the menstrual cycle that stimulates your ovaries to grow follicles, which will hopefully contain an egg. Progesterone causes the endometrium (womb lining) to thicken to prepare for a fertilised egg to implant.

infertility at work. A few weeks later, my GP called to say that my FSH was raised and that I was being referred to the local gynaecology department. They also requested that James did a sperm sample, so all the results would be ready to be reviewed by the gynaecologist.

Having assumed the problem would be mine, and not James', I wasn't fazed by this. James felt otherwise. His request form stated that he had to supply a fresh sample, delivered to the local hospital within an hour of production. There would be nowhere on site to produce the sample. They advised keeping it warm, at around body temperature, by carrying it in a pocket or close to the skin during transport.

Needless to say, it was a stressful morning for James. He wisely chose to complete the task while I was at work, so he didn't have the added pressure of me obsessing over the delivery of his sample. I'm not sure how he felt driving through South-east London with a pot of his semen in his top pocket, but I'm sure it was memorable.

After a few months, the consultation with the gynaecologist came around. We nervously drove to the local hospital and, after stewing in the waiting room for over an hour, we were eventually called in. The doctor sat us down and looked through our results. James' results were completely normal, so after that no further questions were asked in his direction. The whole focus was on my reproductive system.

He explained that my FSH was raised and my anti-Müllerian hormone (AMH) was low for my age, meaning I was heading towards menopause.* From my own research, I knew that the combination of raised FSH and low AMH was a condition called low ovarian reserve. This meant that time was running out before I began to show signs of perimenopause. My days of producing good-quality eggs were limited, and time was of the essence. To achieve the best

---

* Anti-Müllerian hormone is a hormone released from the follicles in the ovary and can indicate a person's egg reserve. It can also indicate how well a person might respond to IVF treatment.

outcome, we were recommended to start IVF. Except they couldn't do that straight away.

Firstly, they would need to check for any physical abnormalities in my womb and ovaries. The doctor recommended a laparoscopy – an operation where a camera inspects the inside of the abdomen or pelvis to check for structural or physical problems. I agreed that I would be happy to undergo this procedure. Then casually the doctor dismissed us from his room by informing us that there was currently a nine-month waiting list for a laparoscopy, and then a further nine-month waiting list for a follow-up. We stood up, thanked the doctor for his time and left the room, stunned.

Eighteen months. Eighteen months before we would even get a referral to a fertility clinic, let alone get on the waiting list at the clinic itself. Eighteen months of seeing my period arrive like clockwork. Eighteen months of trying to keep a grasp on my fragile wellbeing, mine and James' marriage and the future we so desperately wished for.

My heart broke. I already felt like I had waited an eternity for our baby, and now I was being asked to wait even longer. After the appointment I was so shocked that for a few weeks I didn't know what to do. I contemplated waiting for the appointment to come through. I questioned whether we (mainly me) had the patience to go through the hope/grief cycle that came round each month for over a year. I began to look into having the laparoscopy privately, so I could speed up the process.

During my research, I had found a document from my local Clinical Commissioning Group (CCG), which explained the criteria for an IVF referral on the NHS. I did not meet the criteria, as my AMH was too low. This only cemented the decision that we would pursue private treatment. I was relieved as I imagined the heartbreak I would feel having waited for the laparoscopy and follow-up, only to be told that my local CCG wouldn't fund IVF for us anyway. All those months would have been wasted, while my egg reserve dwindled. I felt betrayed by the gynaecologist, who would have known the criteria for referral, and would have been aware that we wouldn't have been eligible. I was deeply wounded and angry. I felt we had been fobbed off.

In the end, after much discussion, James and I knew that we just could not wait any longer for a baby. We had wanted to start a family years before and were still empty-handed, so the thought of waiting even longer felt too much to bear. We decided we would have private treatment with a fertility clinic. We had a modest amount in savings, which meant we were in a fortunate enough position to embark down the road of private fertility treatment. Deciding to go private, although daunting, put the power back into our hands. We had agency to choose which clinic we wanted, and which doctor we wanted to work with. I thanked my lucky stars that we had just enough money to go privately for one round of IVF. Without those savings our dream of having a baby would have been in tatters.

I began researching clinics that might be suitable for treatment. I felt like a total novice, with no idea what to expect and what I should be looking for. It felt like I was cheating on the NHS by going privately, but I just couldn't wait any longer. Clinics all like to share their success rates on their websites, trying to get you to believe that you will be most likely to take home a baby if you sign up with them. The websites have photographs of bouncing, smiling babies, which hit me right in the ovaries. The photos would call to me. I wanted one of those. A giggling, chubby baby to call my own.

Choosing a clinic is one of the most important parts of the IVF journey. For those who win the postcode lottery and receive NHS funding for IVF, your choices are likely to be limited to one or two clinics. Across the country there are varied provisions for IVF, with some areas offering three rounds on the NHS, others one, and in some areas no funding for IVF is provided at all. For those of us footing the bill ourselves, the world is our oyster. Knowing where to start is often the hardest part. I had heard of certain fertility clinics, but on further investigation I had barely touched the tip of the iceberg. Living in London at the time meant that the number of options available to us was vast. On top of that, I had very little knowledge of what IVF actually involved. I didn't know anything about the protocols used,[*] the drugs, what was normal, what wasn't normal. We were about to put all our savings into one big gamble, and we had no idea what was a good bet or not. We knew we would have enough money for one round of IVF only, and on average IVF takes three rounds to be successful. We didn't have a back-up plan for if that one cycle failed, but we were so desperate we were going to take the risk anyway.

One thing I have learnt over the years is that clinics can be very clever about how they display their success rates. They might claim to have a high pregnancy rate, when in fact, if you delve deeper, they are only displaying the success rate per embryo transferred, rather than per cycle undertaken. Clinics might be cancelling cycles on women who don't respond as well to treatment in order to bolster their success rates. Or they may only be showing results for women aged under thirty-five. Or clinics may also have strict criteria of who they accept for treatment, only taking on patients who are likely to have the most success.

In my opinion, the best place to go if you want an unbiased look at the clinic data is the Human Fertilisation and Embryology Authority (HFEA). This is the government regulator for fertility clinics in the UK. They are responsible for inspecting clinics and providing licences. They also hold unbiased data on the success rates of each clinic and can sort them by different variables: age, success per cycle, success per transfer and so on. Although statistics are looking

---

[*] There are various IVF protocols that dictate which drugs will be used, and how long the IVF cycle will last.

at a whole population, rather than your individual chance of success, they are a good place to start.

That said, over the years the statistics have become far less important to me. As someone with a low egg reserve, many clinics would be reluctant to treat me, as my chance of success was far lower and therefore would skew their statistics. Therefore, a clinic which has lower success rates might be more suitable for me as an individual, as they are willing to take the challenge of treating someone with a presumed lower chance of success.

Most clinics will hold open evenings. These are free events where you attend the clinic and listen to a short presentation from the staff. This usually includes what fertility treatments they offer, their success rates (as already mentioned, take these with a pinch of salt), their prices and general information about the clinic. These events also give you the opportunity to see the clinic, talk to the staff and get a feel for the service they offer.

After extensive internet research, there was one clinic that I felt was the right fit for us. I signed us up to the open evening, and after work one evening James and I went along. We were shown to a meeting room full of other couples. There was coffee, tea and snacks available, and then we were encouraged to sit and listen to the presentation. Looking around, we were easily the youngest couple in the room by quite a way, which felt intimidating. There were women attending on their own and couples in their mid-thirties. Some people were there to hear about egg freezing, others IVF and other fertility treatments. The doctor was kind, and his presentation was informative and interesting. We left with an information pack, and the sense that this was the right place for us. I booked us a consultation immediately.

Within two weeks we were sitting in the waiting area of our clinic, listening for our names to be called. The clinic was exceptionally busy; upwards of twenty other people would be waiting every time we went there. Very few men were in the waiting room – a handful at most. It was mainly women, and lots of them. I was shocked at the turnover of people who were entering and leaving the waiting area. It seemed like a conveyor belt. Having never been unwell or had any medical procedures before this point, I wasn't sure what I was letting myself in for.

Waiting has never been my strong point. I sat there tensely, listening out for my name to be called and feeling anxious about what we were going to face. Would we be taken seriously? Did we have a chance at a family? Could we afford to go down this route? How would we tell our families? What if it didn't work? The list of questions racing through my mind went on and on.

Eventually we were taken into the consultation room by a kindly gentleman, probably in his sixties. He smiled and began to ask us about our medical histories. Prior to attending on that day, we had filled in a history form, which was extensive. Pages and pages of questions about our health and medical history. James had a few lifestyle questions to answer, but the bulk of the questions were aimed at me. Details of my menstrual history, obstetric* history, lifestyle and medical problems were all dutifully filled in on this form, only for us to repeat most of the information again in the appointment. James and I consider ourselves to be fit and healthy, both never having had any serious medical problems. We didn't smoke, barely drank, and by this point I was cooking everything from scratch using only organic ingredients. We both exercised, walked the dog and had physical jobs where we would be on our feet most of the day. On paper, there didn't seem to be any red flags as to why we hadn't succeeded in making a baby so far.

The doctor quickly explained that he thought the best route for us would be to try IVF due to my low ovarian reserve. He recommended a protocol and explained the medication to me. He

---

* The medical field of pregnancy, birth and the postnatal period.

said we could start straight away on my next period. I was stunned at how quickly the process was going. We had only self-referred two weeks before and were being told that we could get started straight away. I was excited, but also terrified. The doctor seemed mostly positive due to my age. I can imagine that from his perspective, we were the exception rather than the norm.

I explained that the NHS gynaecologist had recommended a laparoscopy, which made the doctor laugh. He saw no need for this surgery and said that given my age we had a really good chance of having a baby through IVF. He thought it was an unnecessarily invasive surgery. Then he said something I will never forget:

'You are young, you can have as many babies as you want.'

We might be able to have more than one baby. Although this was music to my ears, I was dubious. How could he give such assurances? James, ever the optimist, could only see the positives. This man, who was an expert in fertility treatment, thought that we would be able to have a baby.

The overwhelming feeling when we left the clinic was optimism. We intensely wanted a baby, and here was a man saying that he could help us with that. We wouldn't have to wait another few years; someone was willing to give us a shot right now.

We were due to go on holiday the following week, and then could start our cycle the week after that. We walked out of the clinic with information about our protocol, details of the medication I would be taking and a spring in our step. Perhaps we would have a family after all.

6

Small Talk

Before my own infertility and loss journey, I was completely guilty of asking inappropriate questions. I thought nothing of asking a recently married colleague if they were planning to have children. I didn't know any better and couldn't imagine that these questions would be hurtful in any way. I thought it was an acceptable topic for small talk. It seemed so normal to me, as surely everyone had children shortly after getting married? That was how the Life Plan worked. Once you had ticked one thing, you moved on to the next. Having now been on the receiving end of probing questions, I know first-hand how excruciatingly painful it can be to summon up a response.

So why is it that we choose to ask big questions in small talk? I think I've been asked some of the most personal questions during such episodes of casual chit-chat.

Talking to a new person can be difficult, and finding things to ask about or say can be excruciating when the conversation doesn't flow easily. Outside of work, I find small talk quite difficult as often I don't know what to say. When I'm at work it's a completely different story. I find it easy to strike up a conversation with someone I have only just met. It's part of the job and helps to put the patient at ease in your company. It's a skill I've had to hone over the years. I learnt questions that were good conversation starters: 'Do you know the sex of this baby?' 'Have you packed your hospital bag yet?' 'Have you decided on a name for the baby?' – all aimed at relaxing the patient while they were in hospital.

'Do you have any children?'

This question, I am certain, is never asked out of spite. Quite the opposite. It is seen as an ice breaker. To the average person, this gentle question is so innocent that it almost seems impossible that it could cause offence. Except it can, and it does. It is an incredibly loaded question. I have found that people who ask that question are usually expecting a positive response. It's considered a good conversation starter, as there can be follow-up questions, including how old the children are, where they go to school, what year they are in, what they excel at – and so the list goes on.

When the answer is no, where does the conversation go from there?

If someone appears to be of childbearing age but has no children, I've been guilty of wondering why. It is absolutely none of my business, and there are innumerable reasons why someone might not have a child. My brain wants to know the reason why. It feels as though there is often deep suspicion surrounding women who have not borne children.

At work, I found questions about children particularly poignant, as I felt there was a narrative that implied you couldn't be a good midwife if you didn't have children. This is something I fundamentally disagree with. You can be a truly excellent midwife without ever having been pregnant yourself. To be a good midwife, you need to have empathy. That isn't handed out when you get two pink lines on a pregnancy test. On top of that, all pregnancies are different, so just because a midwife may have been pregnant herself, it doesn't mean she will understand the unique experiences of a patient. Being compassionate and kind are the main ingredients that make a good midwife. Yet still, I felt I had to work even harder than everyone else to prove that I was a competent midwife, as I hadn't lived through pregnancy and birth myself.

As a student I spent a few weeks working in the gynaecology department shadowing the nurses there. I was working with a urogynae nurse, who would specialise in conditions such as urinary incontinence and prolapse. Ethel was one of the patients we saw that day. She was in her eighties and had been brought to the clinic with a prolapse.* She had been brought in by her niece, who waited outside during the appointment. Ethel was having treatment for her prolapse, and the next option she was trying out was a ring pessary, which is a silicone device inserted into the vagina, which holds the vaginal walls in place. Once the examination was concluded, the nurse left the room to collect an information leaflet, leaving me and Ethel alone. I hate sitting in awkward silence, so I decided to start up a conversation with Ethel. She asked about my studies, and I told her I was a student midwife. She seemed to show an interest in this, so I asked Ethel if she had any children of her own. I had assumed that perhaps due to her prolapse she may have experienced pregnancy at some point.

It turned out that Ethel had no children. She had wanted children, but she never found anyone to settle down with. She said she had some nieces and nephews who she was incredibly fond of; they were adults and had children of their own by now. She said it was one of her life's deep regrets that she never had her own, but that she was at peace with it now. I was taken aback by this response as I wasn't expecting it. I had just assumed that Ethel would have had children. I didn't know what an appropriate reply was. The nurse returned shortly after, and the conversation was moved on. I thought about Ethel all day, and lots afterwards. Many years had passed since

---

* A prolapse is when one or more of the pelvic organs drops down from its normal position and bulges into the vagina.

Ethel was able to have children, and yet it still hurt her that she had not become a mother. Over the years I wondered if I would end up like Ethel. I didn't want my life to be tinged with sadness and regret.

Women without children are often portrayed in the media, literature and film as cold or career focused. Take Lady Macbeth – a childless woman who is depicted as power hungry and callous – Miss Hannigan in Annie or poor, 'sad' Jennifer Aniston, who has made the cover of thousands of magazines, with headlines wondering if she will produce a child. Speculation on the contents of a celebrity's womb seems totally normal gossip (while men somehow seem to avoid the same scrutiny). And people are interested – if it wasn't a topic that people wanted to hear about, the magazines wouldn't sell.

The question on everyone's lips is 'Why?' Surely someone could never choose to live a life without children? So there must be something wrong with her instead. There needs to be a justification for the childless state. Despite my own personal experiences, I sometimes find myself wondering why someone hasn't got children, and then I have to remind myself that it is none of my business.

When faced with my own childlessness, I questioned whether I needed to justify myself to others. Desperate to make myself more likeable, I wondered if explaining the truth would make me more endearing to the other person. I don't have children because we've been trying for years. I don't have children because we are doing IVF. Baring these secrets to a stranger felt out of the question, when for a long time we couldn't even tell our closest friends or family. I often didn't have the strength to start an in-depth conversation with a relative stranger. My most often used response would be: 'Not yet.'

Since being on the receiving end of these awkward feelings, I also began to think about all the other situations in which this question could be hurtful. Friends who had yet to meet their significant others, and were watching the days pass by, longing for a family. Friends who were going through miscarriages – managing to get pregnant, only to lose the baby weeks later. Women who don't want to have children at all – a completely valid choice, but one you might not feel like explaining to a person you have only just met. There are myriad reasons why that question, although asked innocently, might make the recipient feel awkward or embarrassed.

Now I am prepared with alternative ice breakers. 'Where do you live?' 'Do you have any hobbies?' 'What are you interested in?' and my personal favourite, 'Tell me something about yourself.' This allows the person to choose what they disclose to you. They might tell you about their job, about their pet horse, about their painting hobby, that they went for a weekend away last month and loved the area. It is a broad, open-ended question, which puts the control with the person answering the question. They can select what they share, with less pressure. Being British, I would also say that, if all else fails, an excellent subject for small talk is the weather – totally inoffensive, and something everyone can relate to or have an opinion about. The point is, there are so many more interesting things we can learn about another person than their parental status.

Similarly, there are certain phrases that get thrown around with the aim of 'helping' when infertility is discussed. Offered as well-meaning advice, things like 'it will happen when you least expect it' and 'just relax' will not be well received. Nothing strikes rage into the infertile person more quickly than hearing these niceties.

Encouraging them to relax implies that the infertile person is in fact trying too hard to have a baby, when I'm not sure you really can try too hard. I WAS relaxed when I first started trying for a baby. As the months ticked by, it became harder and harder to act breezy about the whole situation. You wouldn't dare suggest to someone that they 'just relax' to cure their ear infection, so I'm not sure why it is a suitable suggestion for my ovaries. After a year of trying, I was no longer expecting a pregnancy each month, and was used to the disappointment of my period showing up. I'd been 'not expecting' this for quite some time, and it still hadn't made any difference to the outcome. I have to remind myself that phrases like that are said with nothing but the best intentions. It is never said with malice, yet it greatly undermines the experience of people struggling with fertility issues. Infertility is so deeply misunderstood, and people like to be able to fix problems.

Infertility is defined by the World Health Organization as a disease of the reproductive system. Like many invisible conditions, it is difficult to recognise that someone may be struggling if they are able to go about their day-to-day life as normal. Contrary to popular belief, stress does not cause infertility. Women conceive and birth babies all around the world in incredibly awful conditions. In war zones, refugee camps, famines and so on. Having worked with women for many years, I am assured of the strength that they possess. Women are quite remarkable. If it were the case that stress caused infertility, entire populations would cease to reproduce given the immense stress and hardships that some families endure. Although we can all agree that less stress in our lives is for the best, telling someone the reason that they have yet to conceive a child is due to stress will not help. Instead, you would pile on more guilt and shame, amplifying feelings that are already engulfing us.

Over the years, as I was going through my tumultuous journey to motherhood, I remember also repeatedly being advised to 'just adopt'. Putting 'just' in front of any sentence really minimises the experience of the other person, as though I could just pop down to the local supermarket, pick out a baby of my choosing and then bring it home. The 'just' makes it seem so easy – why hadn't I thought about doing that before? Except I had thought about it. During my years of infertility, I imagined just about every which way it was possible to procure a baby: natural conception, IVF, ICSI,* donor

---

* Intracytoplasmic sperm injection – where the sperm is injected directly into the egg, whereas in IVF the egg and sperm are left in a Petri dish to fertilise by themselves.

eggs, donor sperm, surrogacy, adoption. You name it, I investigated it in great detail. Infertility gives you lots of time to contemplate your childlessness, and how you view your future. James and I decided early on that we weren't particularly keen to live a life without children. So however we got there, we would build a family.

Adopting a child is not a snap decision. For the majority of infertile couples it's not as simple as trying to have sex for a year or two, then, when that doesn't work, picking a baby out of a catalogue. Adoption has its own challenges. Submitting paperwork, being interviewed by social workers and panels to assess your suitability, having your finances scrutinised, getting testimonials from friends and family members and so on. It isn't something you can do on a whim, and you have to be wholly committed to the process. For reasons which I fully understand, many boroughs won't accept you onto an adoption process for sometimes around a year after you have finished trying to conceive. These journeys can't run simultaneously, as they are so very different. You have to fully commit to either one, and then give it your all.

Adoption can also be a long and taxing process. James and I never ruled out adoption, and I researched it extensively, but having gone so far down the fertility treatment route, the thought of having to start again at the beginning of another long process seemed daunting. It is not wrong to want to experience pregnancy and have a child that is related to you. That was something I was keen to try to pursue for our family, and I don't feel ashamed of that. It is, of course, a privilege to bring up a child, but it shouldn't be a privilege to want something that most other couples get to do for free and without the heartache.

I also refute the idea that children waiting for adoption are the responsibility of people without children. Adopting a child is an incredibly worthwhile thing to do, but it is not limited to those of us whose ovaries don't work – any family can extend in this way. It is an entirely different venture to being pregnant, giving birth and raising that child. There are plenty of families who have biological children, who then go on to adopt, as there is no set couple or family that is right for adoption. It is a completely unique journey to creating a family.

For a long time I struggled with desperately wanting to be like everyone else – wanting to have the magical, spontaneous conception, the glowing pregnancy, the straightforward birth and the rosy-cheeked, smiley baby. It is normal to want what you see other people having so easily. You do not need to feel guilty for wanting this, too. When I was told to consider adoption, I then felt guilty for putting so much time, energy and money into pursuing fertility treatment. It felt that my emotions were being belittled, as if they were saying I could fix the problem simply and quickly (an untruth, as the adoption process is anything but quick) but was choosing not to.

7

Sophie – 2, IVF – 0

After a much-needed holiday in Greece, we arrived home and were booked in for an appointment at our clinic to prepare us for starting IVF. While away we had talked about friends who had boasted that they went on holiday and came back pregnant, or that they knew a friend of a friend whose cousin's hairdresser's daughter was about to start IVF and miraculously conceived just before. I secretly hoped that we would be one of those couples, but no such luck for us. At our appointment with the nurse, we had to sign pages and pages of consent forms detailing what would happen to our leftover embryos if we died, if only one of us died, if we separated or one of us changed our mind. All the things you never thought you would need to consider as you embarked on a path to pregnancy and parenthood. The nurse went through the protocol, explaining what medication I would be taking on each day and how to administer it. We left with a prescription to take down to the pharmacy and collect all the drugs I would need.

Unbeknown to me at the time, you can source your drugs from alternative pharmacies to see if cheaper options are available, but instead we headed to the pharmacy on the ground floor and paid close to £2,000 for two huge bags of drugs. The drugs were handed over in green plastic bags, complete with sharps bins to put the used needles in. I carried them into the office and hid them under the desk, hoping none of my colleagues would notice them. Later in the afternoon my team headed into the hospital for a meeting before going home, so I had no choice but to carry them on the bus with us. Colleagues asked what was in the bags, to which I replied, 'Medication,' and swiftly changed the subject.

The next week I began taking all this medication for our first round of IVF. I was doing a long protocol, which, as it implies, takes a few weeks. There are various types of IVF protocol, imaginatively called long or short protocols depending on how long they take. The long protocol involves something called 'down-regulating'. The medication switches off your ovaries and puts you in an artificial state of menopause. This might seem counterintuitive, but when you move on to the next stage of IVF – stimulation – it ensures your ovaries and the follicles are all starting from the same place, reducing the risk that some follicles will develop more quickly, leaving others behind. There are various ways of doing this, and I was on a nightly injection. This was started around day twenty-one of my cycle, ready to start the stimulating drugs once my period arrived.

Much of the medication needs to be mixed to the correct dose; it doesn't come ready made. Powders and solutions are mixed together, and then you extract the amount you need into a tiny syringe and inject it usually into the fatty parts of the body. Being a trained midwife, I knew how to administer medication, but injecting myself was a whole new ball game. The one thing I was sure about was that I would be the one to do it, not just because I didn't trust James with a needle, but also as an act of regaining control of my reproductive destiny.

I checked and double checked the amount of medication I needed to take and then stood there. Was I really about to inject myself? After all the months of waiting, finally I was actually going to be doing something that might get me close to having a baby. I pinched a section of my stomach and put the needle in. I barely felt a thing. I breathed a sigh of relief. I was going to be able to do this.

I began counting down the days until my period arrived, due in a week's time. Once it had, it would mean I could move on to the next stage of the IVF cycle: stimulation. After a year of dreading my period each month, all of a sudden I was desperate for it to arrive. The day it came I called my clinic and informed them, having never felt this excited to see my period before. They booked me in for a scan the next day. James and I hugged and both felt a sense of nervous apprehension. This was a step up in the intensity of treatment, when the real action started.

I had started work as a community midwife in South-west London a few weeks previously. I had informed my new manager that we would be undertaking IVF, and she was incredibly understanding. She let me know that we could fit any appointments around work and told me not to worry. This was a huge relief to me; it was incredible to know I had another source of support. We had told our parents we were doing IVF but hadn't confided in anyone else. I was happy not to be doing shift work at this point. The toll of not sleeping, combined with the long hours, alongside the stress of this huge undertaking might have proved too much for me. I feel so fortunate that I have been surrounded by extremely understanding colleagues, as having the support of my workplace made a huge difference to the mental load I was carrying.

I headed to my clinic first thing in the morning for the internal scan. Sometimes called a baseline scan, this is to check that the lining of the uterus is thinning due to the period, and to make sure there are no cysts and that the follicles that contain the eggs in the ovaries are of a small size. I was not entirely used to internal scans at this time, despite having had a few, and was absolutely horrified and disgusted at the thought of having one while on my period. Thankfully the bleeding was light on this day, but I still could not rid myself of the embarrassment. As a healthcare professional, I know first-hand that doctors, nurses and midwives are completely unfazed by this. We see all manner of bodily fluids on a daily basis, and yet when it came to my own I felt mortified. Now, having been through this process many more times, I'm still not entirely comfortable with other people seeing my bodily fluids, but I know that it is all part of the job and the staff don't bat an eyelid.

The sonographer was a true professional, and the scan was pain-free and over in seconds. I quickly dressed and left the room, after being told I was ready to start the next stage of injections that night. This is the stimulation phase of IVF. The hope is that the stimulating injections encourage several follicles to grow, instead of the usual one that develops in the menstrual cycle. These eggs can then be collected, mixed with the partner's sperm, and ideally transferred back into the womb five days later. At most clinics, this process counts as one IVF cycle.

I felt so lucky that the IVF clinic was in my patch, meaning it was only a short distance away from the community centre my team was based in. It meant minimal disruption to my working day, and I could keep my treatment hidden from my colleagues. I felt like I was walking round with a little secret. I would visit mums with their newborn babies, and for the first time in months I felt like it could be possible that I would get one, too. I was still a very long way away from having a baby, but I felt such a sense of connection with my growing follicles. One of these tiny growths could eventually become a baby of my own.

I visited the home of one lady whose baby had been conceived via IVF. She was so beautiful and happy when she opened her front door. She was dressed head to toe in white, which I thought was unusual (and slightly brave) for someone who had given birth only days earlier. I mentioned that I had read in her notes that this baby was an IVF baby, and she beamed with pride. They had undergone what felt like every test and treatment imaginable. This was to be their final attempt, and by some miracle it had worked, and their baby boy was finally here. She repeatedly said that she couldn't believe her luck, and it was clear that this baby was adored. I was filled with hope after hearing her story. If other people could beat the odds, then perhaps we could, too.

I quickly fell into the routine of IVF. Scan first thing in the morning at 8 a.m. as the clinic opened, either daily or on alternate days, followed by blood tests every other day. I could be on time to start work at 9 a.m., then set off to start my visits round South-west London, before heading home to give myself the two injections. The scans and bloods would monitor the size of the growing follicles in my ovaries. At each scan, my follicles would be counted and measured and then plotted on a graph until they reached a suitable size for extraction. After a week or so of stimulating injections, I was told that the growth was very slow. So slow that in fact a solitary follicle appeared to be growing.

I was devastated. I left the clinic, called James and cried. I had visions that this round of IVF would be cancelled, and we would be told that IVF wasn't an option for us, leaving us childless. I managed to wipe away my tears by the time I reached the office and put on my midwife head as I left for my visits that day. Weighing and checking on the babies seemed harder than usual with the weight of my worst fears present, too. The newborn smell was both intoxicating and repulsive. I sobbed as I walked between visits and would then plaster a smile on my face as I was invited into the new parents' homes. That evening I went for an acupuncture appointment and cried for the full hour while on the couch. After nearly two weeks of injections, only one follicle was growing. It felt like another nail in the coffin; I'd failed to conceive a child, and now I was failing at IVF on the very first attempt.

Back at work the next day, it was my turn to be on call that night. In my team we would take it in turns to be on call for home births in pairs. Around two nights a month we would keep our work phone on in case someone went into labour, and if that happened, we would attend the birth. I left work that evening knowing that I would be called out – I just had a feeling. I laid out clothes in preparation and made sure my phone was on loud so I would hear the call. I headed to bed early to catch as much sleep as I could. In a way, it was a welcome distraction from analysing my insides. With every tiny twinge, I tried to convince myself that my follicles were growing nice and big. Fortunately, the thought of attending a homebirth – something so special – drew my attention away from my ovaries.

Around midnight my phone rang. It was my on-call partner. A second-time mum was in labour, and it sounded like it was progressing quickly. I threw on my clothes, called a taxi, which arrived a few minutes later, and dashed across London. I found the address: it was a flat above a fancy coffee shop and deli, which it turned out the mother and her partner owned. The flat was split level, and upstairs they had knocked all the walls down, so it was one enormous bedroom with an en-suite. They had a floor bed where the whole family slept, and this was where I found my colleague kneeling.

I've always found homebirths to be very special, and this one was no different. My on-call partner had arrived a few minutes before me, and I arrived just as the baby was being born. A little girl, fresh, pink and screaming, had entered the world, while her older brother slept soundly in the same bed next to the mum. The dad went downstairs for a nap shortly after the baby arrived and it felt like a quiet, secret moment. The whole world was sleeping, and we had witnessed a new life entering the world.

The placenta took its time to come, but after some stitches and a round of tea and toast we were nearly ready to leave. Mum was lying in bed, breastfeeding her daughter and looking absolutely radiant. We cleaned up as much as we could, made sure that mum and baby were both comfortable and fed, then headed to the hospital to restock the kit, dispose of used equipment and write up our notes. I glanced at my watch – it was 6 a.m. I was due for a scan at my clinic at 8.30. I typed an email to my clinic explaining that I might be a little late, and also texted my team to say that I had been called out all night so wouldn't be coming in that day.

Fuelled by more tea and toast, we managed to get all the jobs done, and I rushed out of the door. I felt quite grubby by this point, as I hadn't showered and had only had a couple of hours' sleep. I grabbed some breakfast – a protein pot, as I'd read on various IVF forums that eating lots of protein during the stimulation phase can help with follicle growth – and I stumbled to the clinic, getting there just in time.

Jill, the sonographer, loved hearing the story that I had been out all night. To my absolute amazement, during the scan we found that now four follicles were growing and were all becoming a good size. I couldn't believe it. It felt like some of the magic from the homebirth had rubbed off on me. Compared to many women, four is still a very small number, but to me it felt like I had won the lottery. Perhaps I wasn't failing at IVF after all. As the follicles appeared to have reached the desired size, I was given instructions on when to take the trigger shot later that evening. This is the injection that matures the follicles, ready for egg collection thirty-six hours later. I headed home and fell into a deep sleep for the rest of the day, feeling pleased. A lot can change in twenty-four hours.

This was when the nerves really started to kick in. I had never been put to sleep before and it was something I feared. For egg collection I knew I would be heavily sedated, and the thought petrified me. I remember walking from the station to the clinic, holding hands with James and wondering if I would ever wake up from the anaesthetic. Although I had worked in a hospital for many years, in maternity we rarely put people under general anaesthetic. I was fearful of the process and at the thought of being unconscious while other people were in charge of my body. Was I putting my life at risk unnecessarily? It felt like we were in too deep at this point. We had paid for the cycle and the drugs. I'd completed nearly four weeks of injections – there was no turning back now. I so desperately wanted a baby, so I decided this was a risk I was willing to take.

We walked into the clinic waiting room and were told to take a seat. Before long we were taken upstairs into what looked more like a hotel room but was in fact a hospital room. It had a view of the riverside park opposite, and there were wooden wardrobes, a flat-screen television and a welcome pack. I had worked some shifts on the private maternity ward but couldn't believe I was being treated to similar facilities myself.

The nurse, doctor and anaesthetist all came to see me and prep me for the morning's procedure. Then, while I waited for my turn to go down to theatre, the catering staff came to give me a menu, from which I chose three courses. No wonder the price was so expensive – it was beginning to feel more like a holiday than an appointment for an invasive procedure. I was given an expensive disposable heated gown to put on – a step up from the usual hospital gowns I would give out to patients.

James was served coffee and biscuits, and then after a while he was called down to the lab to provide his sample, which would be used to fertilise any eggs that were collected. This part of the process had been weighing heavily on my mind, thankfully more than it had been on James'. He was instructed to go downstairs, collect a pot, then, once in the designated room, he would provide a semen sample and put it through a small hatch in the wall for collection by the lab technicians. Having spent the previous year scouring websites and forums, I was acutely aware that at this point nerves can get the better of partners far more frequently than is ever spoken about. Considering that the

IVF process isn't really talked about, trying and failing to produce a semen sample is talked about even less. The pressure to perform can be overwhelming during what can already be a stressful day. I didn't want to put even more pressure on James by letting him know that I was nervous, so I anxiously wished him luck as he left. Thankfully, James managed his sample without any trouble, although on exiting the room he realised he had forgotten to lock the door!

Shortly after, I was walked down to the theatre. At this point I began to shake with fear. I was sitting on the trolley while the anaesthetist and assistant checked my name and began getting the medication ready. They made idle chit-chat to distract me, but I was completely terrified. A cannula was inserted into my hand, and then the doctor came in to perform a quick internal scan to make sure I hadn't already ovulated. Once it was confirmed that all the follicles remained, an oxygen mask was placed over my face and the anaesthetist reached for a syringe of white liquid, which was slowly inserted through the cannula into my veins. I stared at the ceiling and drifted off into the most peaceful sleep.

'How many eggs did I get?' were the first words I uttered as soon as I woke up from the sedation.

I was in the recovery bay with other patients – not just IVF patients, but anyone who'd had an operation that day. I was awake, and feeling warm and cosy, having had the most wonderful sleep. The nurse came over and checked my observations, before telling me that seven eggs had been collected. Seven! This was beyond anything I had anticipated. I was eggstatic (sorry, I couldn't resist). Not only had the anaesthetic been a wonderful, relaxing experience, but hearing that I had produced far more eggs than I ever thought possible was just fantastic. Compared to a few days earlier when I'd been convinced IVF would never work for us, here I was grinning from ear to ear. I was wheeled back up to my room where James was waiting for me, and I could barely contain my excitement.

I look back on this day so fondly, as I finally found some hope that perhaps things were going to be okay. The whole day I felt tremendously well looked after. After spending years caring for other people, it felt so reassuring to receive great care from some truly kind and compassionate doctors and nurses. I napped some more, and when I was feeling more awake I was brought a three-course lunch. I have always loved my food, even as a tiny little girl. And this wasn't your standard hospital food – this was restaurant quality. At this moment in time I had absolutely no regrets about our decision to go private. I was just so thankful that we had a small amount of savings to use. Throughout our entire route to parenthood, this will always be one of my favourite days. It felt like finally something was going our way. I hadn't failed. Maybe IVF was going to work for us.

A few hours later, we were discharged. We called a taxi and headed home. I felt every single bump that the taxi went over but was still so high from the egg collection that I didn't mind. We snuggled up on the sofa with our dog, Crumpet, and ate pizza while watching TV. I started medication that night to prepare my body for the embryo transfer, which would be happening in a few days' time. This medication is progesterone, which is a hormone released during pregnancy. By taking it for a few days before the embryo transfer, your body is getting ready for the embryo to implant, and to support the natural hormones released by the body. There are a few ways progesterone can be administered and the most common one is a pessary. An oily capsule, which you insert either into your vagina or rectum twice a day.

From my time on the antenatal ward, I was very familiar with the progesterone pessaries. Many women would be on them if they were at risk of preterm labour. I had handed them out during the drugs round more times than I could remember, and no patient had ever mentioned to me how unpleasant they were. That evening I inserted the first pessary deep into my vagina and didn't think any further about it. Until the entire thing began to melt and leak out of me. The substance is thick and oily, and it stained or ruined nearly every single pair of underwear that I owned. The feeling of this thick substance leaking out of me was not nice. I tried using panty liners to collect the mess, but that was still unpleasant. I had searched the internet to see if I was doing something wrong and found that the most popular route of entry was the back passage. I was a bit shocked, and in all honesty a little bit grossed out. It was only after another episode of the entire pessary leaking out that I decided to get over my squeamishness and insert them rectally. Having given countless suppositories and enemas over the years, I was still deeply dubious about inserting the medication myself. I sat on the side of the bath for ages, working myself up to doing it. The first few times it felt so uncomfortable, and I was a bit horrified about having to stick my finger in somewhere that was meant to be exit only, but after a few days I realised I had absolutely made the right decision. No more mess, no more discomfort, and I could get on with my day. I would definitely recommend to anyone going through IVF to use the back passage for these. James and I nicknamed them 'bum bullets' due to their shape. Having taken probably close to a thousand of these over the course of a few years, I consider myself a bit of an expert now!

A consistent feature of infertility is waiting. Following egg collection, the waiting begins. You wait to hear from the embryologist the following day to see how many, if any, of the eggs are fertilised. Then you usually wait to hear again from the embryologist on day three to see how the embryos are doing. Then finally, five days after the egg collection, if any of the embryos are still growing the embryologist will select the best-looking embryo and this will be inserted back into the womb.

Those few days between egg collection and transfer are like holding your breath. I jumped every time my phone made a noise, in case it was a call from the clinic letting us know about our little embryos. My egg collection had been on a Friday, and I wasn't working during the weekend, so I had a lazy start to the day, then got up and walked Crumpet. I checked my phone around every fifteen minutes to see if I had somehow missed the call. I kept checking that I had signal and I tried and failed to distract myself. Around lunchtime the embryologist called and informed me that out of the seven eggs collected, four were mature* and had all fertilised. Having spent hours on forums, I was aware that not all the eggs collected would be mature, and not all would fertilise. IVF is very much a numbers game, and you expect the number of embryos to reduce as the days go on. Having seen four good-size follicles in my scans, I wasn't surprised that only four eggs had fertilised. Those extra three eggs that had been collected were a bonus, and likely from some much smaller follicles. Still worth collecting, just in case, but unlikely to result in a baby.

I hung up the phone, and immediately called James and told him the good news. I remember feeling hugely overwhelmed at this point. Cells from James and I had combined and made embryos. They had joined together and taken the very first step to becoming a baby. I was in awe of science, technology and the human body. Every person who has ever existed has started off as an embryo consisting of one egg and one sperm. Knowing that so far we had never got as far as making an embryo together, this felt so very special and momentous.

Infertility makes you think negative thoughts about yourself. At times I had doubted whether James and I were capable of making a baby. Perhaps we were incompatible, and nature was telling us we couldn't be parents together. Now, finally, we had made embryos. The feeling was truly indescribable at the time. A week earlier I was convinced IVF would never work for us, and here were four little embryos growing in a dish.

---

* A mature egg is one that is suitable for fertilisation.

Two days later I received the next phone call saying that all four embryos were going strong and growing well, and therefore my embryo transfer would be booked in for two days' time. I had expected another drop-off, so to hear that all four were still prospering felt incredible. I wished with all my might that they would keep growing for another two days.

The day of the embryo transfer was nerve-wracking. We had been told that if we didn't hear anything further, we could come in for the transfer. If we received a phone call it was likely because none of the embryos had survived and there would be nothing to transfer. I was constantly checking my phone to see if I had missed a call, and every time it buzzed I would jump in fear. No phone call came, so James and I set out from our flat and travelled across London for our embryo transfer.

Instructions from the clinic explained that I should arrive at the clinic with a full bladder. If the bladder is full, it pushes the uterus into a better position, making the transfer easier. I thought to myself, this won't be a problem in the slightest. I only have to look at a glass of water and my bladder is full. We arrived ten minutes early, and I drank an extra swig of water as we sat in the waiting room.

Ten minutes passed and no one called us. Twenty minutes passed and no one called us. Thirty minutes passed, and I was getting more and more agitated. I'm impatient at the best of times, but my full bladder was becoming more and more uncomfortable. I headed to the front desk to find out what was happening, and the receptionist told me that they were running late. In my desperation, I made a break for the loo and tried to empty the smallest amount of urine, while leaving my bladder nice and full for the transfer. I then sat outside and drank a whole bottle of water to make sure it would be full enough in time. In hindsight, this was definitely not my smartest move.

Another thirty minutes of me wriggling around in my chair,

wishing I had spent more time on my pelvic-floor exercises, and we were finally called in. To say I was agitated was an understatement – I'm not sure my bladder had ever been so full before. I was asked to undress from the waist down and then sit on a chair with my legs in stirrups. By now, I was genuinely worried that I might not be able to hold my pee for much longer. James sat beside me holding my hand, and I grimaced in discomfort. They checked mine and James' names and began to prep for the transfer.

A cold metal speculum was inserted into my vagina, and I began to worry about peeing all over the doctor. To add to this growing pressure, a nurse pressed a scanning probe over my tummy and it felt like it was directly on my bladder. The pressure was unbelievable, and I was close to tears. The embryologist passed a catheter through a hatch in the wall, which contained our embryo. The only embryo that had made it this far. Two had stopped growing since our last phone call, and one was not quite big enough to transfer. This was our one chance at a baby.

The catheter was inserted through the speculum, through my cervix and into my womb. On the screen I could see the doctor lining everything up into the perfect position before he released the embryo from the catheter and into my womb. A tiny speck of fluid showed the position of the embryo, and although my bladder was protesting, it still felt like a magical moment.

The moment the speculum was removed, I jumped up and ran off to the toilet. I sat there and wondered whether I was peeing out my hard-won embryo. Had I just flushed £10,000 quite literally down the toilet?

I was told to take a pregnancy test in nine days' time, and that was it. I had to pee again, as my bladder was sore and irritated by this point, and we left clutching a photo of the embryo – a round ball of cells. We stepped outside, said our goodbyes, and then I headed off to work.

I was due to visit a woman about a ten-minute journey from the clinic, so I set off feeling like I was walking around with a secret in my tummy. The woman I visited was tearful and tired, and I spent an hour helping her baby latch on to the breast. I spent a long time checking the baby, but also just staring at it. She was so small and perfect. This baby had started off as an embryo, and now here she was. This was the closest I had ever been to being pregnant. Our little embryo was hopefully getting nice and snuggly inside my womb.

The next nine days passed painfully slowly. I yoyo-ed between thinking it had worked and thinking it definitely had not worked. Every single twinge in my body was a potential pregnancy symptom. I was even imagining nausea, or perhaps I was feeling sick from the nerves.

I find it particularly cruel that as progesterone is a pregnancy hormone, it mimics pregnancy symptoms. Any bloating, constipation or nausea could be attributed to the bum bullets I was inserting twice a day. Overall, I had minimal symptoms, which in itself was both reassuring and worrying.

When running my antenatal clinics, I would stare at the bumps and wonder what it would look like on me. Every time I would palpate my patient's abdomen to feel the position of her baby, I would feel a warmth flood through me. The wriggles and kicks of their baby under my hands would remind me that I had my own little secret within. I hoped that all the oxytocin – the so-called 'love hormone' – that was flowing was making my womb nice and welcoming.

The almost overwhelming temptation to do a pregnancy test early was strong. I never kept any in the house as every time I tested and was faced with one pink line instead of two I would be heartbroken. I would never have betrayed James' trust and bought one in secret, so instead I resisted and counted down the days.

On the eighth day after the embryo transfer I popped into a pharmacy in between home visits to buy the pregnancy test I would need for the next morning. As I stood in the aisle looking at all the tests, I felt a strange sense of apprehension. In less than twenty-four hours we would know if our first IVF attempt had worked. I honestly had absolutely no idea whether one line or two would greet me in the morning. I constantly felt like my body was keeping secrets from me and was impossible to read. This was no different. Was my body growing a tiny baby in there? Or would I be back to square one, except this time several thousand pounds poorer?

I tried my hardest to focus on work and, once home, on distracting my mind.

I laid out the pregnancy test and a pot to pee in all ready for me. It was recommended to use the first urine sample in the morning, as this would allow the pregnancy hormone to build up and ideally show the strongest line on the pregnancy test.

When James and I climbed into bed we held hands, not knowing what to say. I eventually drifted off into a restless sleep. When I woke, I knew it wasn't time to do the test so I tried to ignore the adrenaline that had started to pump through my body. What felt like hours later I turned to look at the clock, only to find that it was 2 a.m. Not time to test yet, so I rolled over, closed my eyes and tried to turn off my brain.

Perhaps it was my body's way of telling me it was time, but the next time I woke I was absolutely desperate for the loo: 4 a.m. Not my preferred wake-up time but needs must. I told James that I couldn't wait any longer, and he agreed that there was no time like the present.

Off I went to the bathroom, suddenly unsure whether this was the right thing to do. I carefully unwrapped the test and balanced it on the side of the bath while I peed into the pot. I then dipped the end of the test into the pot and laid it on the side. I quickly washed my hands and rushed back into bed. James put a three-minute timer on his phone, and we lay there in silence, holding hands, while the longest three minutes of my life ticked by.

Finally, the alarm sounded and the moment of truth was upon us. We both got out of bed and headed into the bathroom. I turned the test over and looked.

Two pink lines.

8

The Twelve-week Rule

If you were thinking that after so long trying for a baby, and after a gruelling round of IVF, that a positive pregnancy test would have us jumping for joy or weeping tears of happiness, then you are mistaken.

We hugged in disbelief, then climbed back into bed and fell into a deep sleep in each other's arms. All the nerves, stress, excitement and worry of the past year, and especially the last month or so, washed over us and could temporarily be forgotten.

I was happy – of course I was; this was everything I had been hoping, wishing, praying for. At the same time it didn't seem real, and the emotional and physical exhaustion had finally caught up with me. The overwhelming emotion was relief. It had worked. We weren't a lost cause. We might get our family after all.

When we eventually woke, we decided to go out in the fresh air and walk Crumpet. I felt no different to the day before, the week before or even the month before. There was absolutely nothing to make me believe that I was pregnant. Just a pregnancy test sitting proudly on my bedside table.

We phoned both sets of parents and told them the good news. As they knew we had been going through the IVF process, it felt right to tell them straight away. They were delighted for us, and it felt great to share our news with them. After the worry of the past few months, we had something positive to tell them.

I know many couples choose not to announce their pregnancies until after the first twelve weeks. This is because the risk of miscarriage after this stage significantly reduces. We had no plans to tell any wider friends or family at this point, but knew we wanted our parents to feel the joy with us, as they had also shared our pain and nerves throughout the IVF process.

I've performed many antenatal booking appointments – the first midwife appointment that a pregnant person will have – and am asked frequently whether it is okay to share the news before twelve weeks. I've even been asked for permission. This has shown me that there is real apprehension around sharing early-pregnancy news. This is due to a fear of talking about pregnancy loss and miscarriage. One in four women will experience miscarriage, so it is not a rarity. And yet there is a real taboo around this topic. The idea behind not mentioning early pregnancy is that if, sadly, a miscarriage was to occur, then you wouldn't have to mention this either.

I can absolutely understand not wanting to share the most intimate details of your life with your entire address book, but I do believe that your nearest and dearest would want to support you through a miscarriage. If you don't tell them you have miscarried, how can they do this?

The advice I give to clients now is: tell who you want, when you want. The inner workings of your body are your business, and your business alone, unless you wish to share them with other people. I believe you should announce your pregnancy whenever you feel ready, whether that is at four weeks or forty weeks. If you want to share the news that you are expecting, then go ahead. Telling people you are pregnant won't have any bearing on the outcome of the pregnancy. Your baby won't die because you dared to tell someone. And on the same note, if you wish to keep the news to yourself for longer than twelve weeks, again it should be a decision for you and your partner (if you have one). It is your body and your baby. If you want to shout across the rooftops that you are expecting, then go ahead. By the same logic, if you want to keep the precious news to yourself, that is okay, too.

Much like how periods are seen as messy, dirty and something not to be discussed, miscarriages are the same. Having never experienced a first-trimester miscarriage myself, I had heard and believed that it was like a heavy period. I now know from listening to women who have lived through it that this is not the case at all. They can be heavy, extremely painful, scary – not least because of the emotional aspect, which can be devastating. The physical side of miscarriage can last for weeks, and can require time away from work. There can be surgery, emotional farewells over the toilet bowl, guilt, fear, regret and more. This unwritten twelve-week rule is outdated and seems to keep pregnancy loss a shameful secret.

The convention of not sharing a pregnancy until twelve weeks seems to have unclear origins, but it could be linked to the introduction of ultrasound scanning. Pregnant people will be offered a scan at around twelve weeks. During this scan the pregnancy is 'dated', which means the sonographer will take several measurements of the baby, as well as note the first day of the last menstrual period, and from that work out the estimated due date of your baby. Ultrasound scanning started being used in the 1960s. Routinely two ultrasound scans are offered during a pregnancy, with more being offered if there are any concerns. Scanning is widespread, with private ultrasound scans available from clinics who charge for all sorts of packages and offers. At the 'dating' scan, alongside working out the due date, the sonographer will check that the pregnancy is located in the womb, how many babies are growing, and will check for basic development. You will also be offered a test to screen for chromosomal abnormalities. It is at this point that it is commonplace for couples to begin to share their news, after having the reassurance that all is well so far.

On one occasion a woman and her partner turned up for their booking-in appointment with the midwife, and she was proudly wearing her 'Baby on Board' badge. The booking-in appointment is the very first midwife appointment where the patient will be asked lots of questions about her medical history and any previous pregnancies so a plan of care can be formulated. The appointment also consists of blood and urine tests, and blood pressure checks, and the midwife will give lots of information regarding pregnancy. On this occasion, the patient was six weeks pregnant. At the time I remember thinking it was unusual but also refreshing to see someone embracing their pregnancy early on. It stood out to me, because it was not the norm. At that stage, it's more often the case that a client is trying to hide her pregnancy folder in her bag before she leaves the room. Neither is right or wrong, just different.

Our pregnancy test was taken at the beginning of December, and we had arranged to visit friends in Lincoln. We decided it would be an excellent distraction if the test was negative, or a great way to make a good weekend even better if the result was positive. We drove up north and spent the weekend visiting the Christmas market. I ordered hot apple juice while the others all drank mulled wine, and pretended it was because I was driving. I was going along with the convention of not letting the news slip.

We came home and on the Sunday evening we put our Christmas decorations up. I allowed myself to imagine next year's Christmas and got butterflies. Before infertility, Christmas had been one of my favourite times of year, but while we were trying unsuccessfully to conceive it was a painful reminder that we were unable to have a baby. I tried to remain level-headed and remind myself that pregnancy took forty weeks, and I was four weeks in, but a ripple of excitement went through my body nonetheless.

On Monday I went back to work, trying to focus my attention anywhere except my womb. I was a mix of emotions: gratitude, apprehension, fear and excitement. On my lunchbreak, I called my clinic to let them know the good news. They congratulated me and booked me in for a scan. I was recommended to have a scan at around six weeks pregnant; however, because the clinic closed over Christmas and New Year, ours was scheduled for seven weeks, making it the first week in January. Yet more waiting. I had completed the two-week wait after the embryo transfer, and now I had three further weeks to find out if there really was a baby inside me.

During a shopping trip with my mum later that week, I mentioned that for my poached egg breakfast, I'd had a double-yolker. We laughed, and she joked that perhaps I was expecting twins. I shrugged this off. I'd only had one embryo transferred, and although twins are more common with IVF, the majority of these are from double embryo transfers. Over the next few days, I began to feel increasingly nervous. At frequent intervals throughout the day, I would go to the bathroom so I could check my underwear for bleeding. I would think that I could feel a wet sensation and convince myself that I was having a miscarriage. During my antenatal clinic, I would dash to the bathroom in between appointments, pull my trousers down to inspect my pants, then dash back so I wouldn't run late. If I was out doing home visits, I began to ask clients if I could use their bathrooms so I could check. A sigh of relief would momentarily flood my body when it was clear that my mind was playing tricks on me.

Until it wasn't.

I had been rushing round all day. As a community midwife working in London, most of my team got around via public transport or on foot. I was a big fan of walking between my visits, as it was good exercise, and exploring London on foot can be magical. At the end of the day, we would all reconvene at the office and sort out any admin.

I went to the bathroom to check for possibly the twentieth time that day, and as I pulled down my underwear there was blood. Brown, and not a lot, but enough for my brain to go into overdrive and predict the worst-case scenario: the end of the pregnancy.

I called the early pregnancy unit (EPU) at the hospital I worked at and explained I was five weeks pregnant with an IVF pregnancy, and I'd had some bleeding. The nurse on the phone was kind and invited me in for a scan first thing the next morning.

After an anxious night, James and I made our way to the EPU. We sat in the waiting room, holding hands, wondering if this was game over for us. Other people left the clinic rooms clutching scan photos, and I wondered if this meant that all the good news had been used up for that day.

We were eventually called into the clinic room. I was asked to undress from the waist down – something I was used to by now – and I lay on the couch for an internal scan. (At this early stage of gestation the uterus wouldn't be visible via an abdominal scan.) The sonographer had faced the screen away from us, and James and I held hands and looked at each other while anxiously awaiting news.

The sonographer and her colleague were friendly and kind, asking us lots of questions about our IVF round. They asked which clinic we went to, when the first day of my last period was, when the embryo was transferred, and then she asked how many embryos we'd had transferred. I answered one, and then continued to lie and wait while she carried on scanning. We chatted about our infertility diagnosis, and how some people do manage to conceive naturally with low ovarian reserve. I appreciated the efforts to distract me, but I was desperate for news.

Strangely the sonographer again asked how many embryos had been transferred. She then turned the screen to face me. Immediately I saw that in the middle of a screen of grey there were two black circles and I squeezed James' hand.

Our only day-five embryo had split in two, and I was pregnant with identical twins.

James was not used to looking at scans, so I had to spell it out for him:

'There's two.'

We left the clinic room with huge grins plastered to our faces and holding our very own scan photo. I just couldn't believe it. Things like this didn't happen to people like me. I couldn't get pregnant, and now there were two babies making a home in my womb. The small, grainy photo that I clutched in my hands meant more than anything else in the world.

At this time, I was five weeks and five days pregnant, so on the scan there wasn't much to see. Two gestational sacs, each with a yolk sac in them. The twins were identical as they came from the same embryo, but they were in separate sacs and would form separate placentas. This was reassuring to hear as typically there were fewer complications with this type of twin pregnancy.

The scan showed that I had a small area of bleeding called a subchorionic haematoma.* Although this is more common in IVF pregnancies, it was uncertain whether it meant the start of a miscarriage or was just an unfortunate scary incident. For the moment, the news of twins had eclipsed all else, and I was caught up in the excitement of it all.

James and I kissed goodbye and both went off to work. I had a postnatal visit round the corner, so I set off on foot and James headed off to his pub. While walking I called my mum to tell her. It felt so surreal. The words were coming out of my mouth, but it felt like I was talking about someone else. My mum called out with excitement and nearly crashed her car!

---

* A subchorionic haematoma is an area of bleeding between the uterus and the amniotic sac.

I vividly remember the postnatal check I completed. Everything seemed so vibrant. Despite being December, the sun was shining and London felt peaceful. I remember the house so clearly, too. Builders were doing work, so I entered via the door on the basement level of a four-storey townhouse. The mum was sitting in the living area, with long brown hair. Her own mother was sitting attentively nearby. I really hoped my mum would be able to do this for me, too. She loved being around babies, and I was sure that, having been a midwife herself, her knowledge would help me if my own brain was caught in a sleep-deprived haze.

I always recommend that parents-to-be say yes to any help that is offered. If you have a good relationship with your parents, or your partner's parents, it can be invaluable to have them nearby. On top of that, it can be a wonderful experience to have grandparents around to get to know their grand-baby. They are usually also great at holding the baby while you and your partner have a quick nap or shower.

The next day I got up and made breakfast. Poached eggs on toast, a favourite of mine. To my surprise there was another double-yolker. Two double-yolkers in the space of a week! This was surely a sign that these twins were meant to be. Smiling to myself, I carried on with my morning routine, but as I was about to leave the house, I felt a familiar warmth in my underwear. More blood. My clinic agreed to scan me again, which showed nothing more than the scan the day before. Two sacs still growing, with an area of bleeding underneath. The sonographer and nurses advised me to sit tight, but my nerves were a mess.

I already felt like I'd run a marathon and I had only found out I was pregnant two weeks ago. I was now six weeks pregnant, and a switch had been turned on. Morning sickness arrived. Having looked after hundreds and hundreds of pregnant women at work, I felt a bit betrayed when I realised that no one had managed to describe to me quite how horrendous it was. It was AWFUL.

I discovered that the reason no one had successfully managed to impress on me how horrid it was, was perhaps because there aren't even words to describe it. I was nauseous from the second I woke up until the second I went to bed, and even during the night. And it wasn't the sort of nausea where you feel a bit off or not quite right. This was all-encompassing. I would retch constantly. I couldn't even leave the house without a plastic bag for fear of throwing up.

Thankfully I wasn't sick every day, but the nausea was completely debilitating. I had to eat constantly, even during the night, because if my stomach was empty the nausea was worse. Having eaten nothing but organic, homemade food for the past few months, all of a sudden I could only stomach beige foods. My bedside table was covered in crackers, biscuits and cake bars as I would wake up several times a night with my stomach churning. I have struggled to put into words quite how bad the nausea was, but I wanted to curl up into a ball for the next few weeks until it was all over.

I tried all the commonly known sickness cures: ginger – including ginger tea, ginger biscuits, ginger sweets – travel sickness bands, dry crackers, peppermint tea, eating little and often, not eating; I tried it all. I'm not a huge ginger fan anyway, so it was never going to cure the twenty-four-seven nausea and vomiting I was experiencing. The only thing that managed to keep a handle on the sickness was boiled sweets, preferably lemon flavoured, and even then it would be touch and go.

At the time, I had a fifteen-minute train commute to work, with a ten-minute walk on either side. This journey became torturous. I would retch on the walk to the station, then I would stand on the platform and start sucking a sweet as soon as the train pulled into the platform. I would then stand, munching my way through as many sweets as I needed while on the train until it was time to get off – praying that I wouldn't need to retch or be sick in the carriage. I would then get my trusty plastic bag out, and retch into it on the walk to the office. When I reached the office, I would put the bag into my pocket and head inside, where I would pretend that I felt completely normal. I am genuinely surprised that I have any teeth left after the number of boiled sweets I ate.

I did this in secret for twelve weeks, as I too had been conditioned not to tell anyone about my pregnancy. Despite feeling on death's door most days, I put on a brave face and pretended I felt completely fine. I'm sure my colleagues guessed, but they didn't say anything.

Christmas came, and I nervously imagined two tiny helpers putting decorations on the tree. I managed a few mouthfuls of my Christmas dinner but was mostly horizontal. New Year passed and we toasted to new adventures next year. And by toasted, I mean we sent each other a nice text message. James was working in his pub, and I was in bed by 9 p.m.

Our next scan was booked for 2 January, and the holidays had been an excellent distraction, but the anxiety was bubbling away. I couldn't sleep for nerves, and the morning sickness was by now so bad that I wondered if I could even make it through the night.

Thankfully, at this scan the two sacs had developed into two tiny people with flickering heartbeats. I'd never seen a more beautiful sight. The bleeding from two weeks previously had disappeared, and our two little blobs were measuring the correct size and were nestled in the correct place.

I was still taking the progesterone pessaries, aka bum bullets, which is normal in IVF pregnancies. Progesterone is a naturally occurring pregnancy hormone, so taking an artificial version encourages implantation and supports the pregnancy for the first trimester. It might have been down to all the medication I was taking, or even a desperation to believe that there really was something going on inside my womb, but the beginnings of a bump began to show early on. Easy to hide with some loose-fitting clothes, or a thick jumper, but I could see a noticeable difference.

When we were trying and failing to make a baby, certain things would really upset me, and one of those was the 'Baby on Board' badge. I absolutely understand why people wear them, but for some reason it felt like a dagger in my heart every time I saw one. It wasn't enough that I could see their blooming abdomen; they had to spell it out to me that they were pregnant and I was not. It's not a feeling I'm particularly proud of, but infertility really does bring up some unattractive feelings. These emotions are all valid, as infertility is one of the most difficult and misunderstood experiences. Because I felt so awful on my commute, however, I did start to wear a 'Baby on Board' badge at around ten weeks of pregnancy. I couldn't bear the packed train any longer, and as the nausea was extreme, I was desperate for a seat. I was quite horrified by myself that I was the person with the badge that might be breaking someone else's heart. I would dread someone asking me how many weeks pregnant I was, in case I had to confess that I was less than twelve weeks, and therefore didn't count as 'properly' pregnant. I can see how silly that sounds, but I believed my pregnancy didn't count until I had made it past the first trimester. As soon as I was off the train, I would take the badge off and hide it in my pocket in case anyone saw me. I thought back to my patient who was proudly wearing her badge from the moment she found out she was pregnant. I wished I could be more like her.

I had my own booking-in appointment at ten weeks with a midwife who I was friends with and had trained with. I had let her know I was pregnant as I wanted her to look after me throughout. She was not only a trusted friend, but a competent midwife, and I felt so safe in her capable hands. It felt strange answering all the questions that I was normally asking. James came with me and sat listening attentively. He had even prepared a question to ask, which I thought was so sweet. My colleague kindly went through all the information for his benefit. She took my bloods, blood pressure, urine sample and did other routine checks. At the end of the appointment, I was given my own pregnancy folder. Having read, written in, carried and inspected hundreds of these folders before, I finally had one of my very own.

I had thought that time moved slowly during the two-week wait after I had my positive test, but time was moving so slowly now it had almost stopped. The retching, vomiting and nausea continued at quite a pace. I made myself go to work every day, I only took one day off in the first trimester after I had walked to the station and vomited down myself. I didn't want to complain or appear ungrateful, as I was deeply, deeply blessed that our very first round of IVF had worked in such a spectacular way.

Now that I knew there were two babies in there, the stakes felt even higher. My pregnancy had shifted into the high-risk category without me even having had the chance to think about it. I had always imagined that I would have a low-risk, straight-forward pregnancy, ending in a calm, positive birth. Twins was a whole different ball game. Carrying more than one baby meant I was at a higher risk of developing gestational diabetes (diabetes in pregnancy), pre-eclampsia (a high-blood-pressure condition of pregnancy), preterm labour, miscarriage, anaemia (low iron levels) and more. I knew it was likely I would be having a caesarean, and that I was unlikely to make it to full term. My due date was August, but I thought July was looking like the most likely month that these twins might make their appearance.

James and I would discuss our plans in whispers, almost feeling embarrassed or guilty for thinking that far ahead. We didn't want to assume that a positive pregnancy test meant we would bring one or two babies home.

At the time, we lived in a two-bedroom flat. We might have been able to squeeze one baby and all the paraphernalia in, but there was no way we would be able to cope with double that and a dog. We were on the first floor, so lugging two babies, a double buggy or car seats up and down the stairs following major surgery to bring them into the world seemed an impossible task.

My anxiety at this point was unreal. My mum urged me to put our flat on the market and start looking at houses, but I couldn't bring myself to. I thought that if I acknowledged the pregnancy then it would jinx it, and I would miscarry these much-longed-for babies. I compromised, agreeing that we would start looking once I was twelve weeks pregnant. I was enforcing the twelve-week rule on myself.

Having been extremely low at points while trying to conceive, I was now constantly on edge. We had gambled nearly every penny we had on making a baby, and the emotional cost was even higher. I felt like I had to prove that I was worthy of this pregnancy. Perhaps there was a reason I hadn't been able to get pregnant in the first place. Maybe I was never meant to be a mother, and by some fluke I had slipped through the net. Once the pregnancy gods noticed, they would realise their error and take my babies away.

I began a series of rituals where I tried to prove that I was worthy of the precious gift I was carrying. Looking back, I can see this was due to the debilitating fear that my babies would be taken away from me. I put it down to this being an IVF pregnancy and having gone through such a lot to get to this point.

I would only sleep on my left side. In the third trimester pregnant women are advised to sleep on their left, as this maximises blood flow to the uterus and therefore the baby. Despite this having absolutely no bearing in the first trimester, I was desperate to show that I was invested in this pregnancy. I wanted to keep these babies safe and do everything within my power to protect them. Every morning in the shower I begged these two babies to keep growing, and I told them how loved they were already.

I began obsessively checking a website that offered a 'miscarriage calculator' (I absolutely do not recommend doing this to yourself, as it will drive you mad). Every day, and sometimes several times a day, I would check this website to see what the chances of me miscarrying on that particular day were. It almost felt like a miscarriage was inevitable for me, as if after so much heartbreak I wasn't allowed to be happy.

I felt really strange sitting there in my antenatal appointments knowing that my patient wasn't the only one growing something inside her; my babies were also with us. I would talk to them in between my appointments. Now, when patients asked if I had any children, I answered no, but it didn't sting quite as much.

The final scan of our first trimester was our dating scan. As this was an IVF pregnancy, we knew the transfer date, and therefore already knew my due date, but I had the scan to check all was progressing well. I left the appointment with yet another scan photo, and a sigh of relief.

I had made it through the first trimester.

9

Hello and Goodbye

'You're pregnant.'

I was taken aback. I had only just taken off my coat and shoes as I had entered a huge apartment in a mansion block near the King's Road to carry out a postnatal check. The new mother must have seen the surprised look on my face.

'You're wearing travel sickness bands.'

I had resorted to these bands in desperation at my continuing pregnancy sickness. I felt embarrassed, as despite now being in the second trimester, I still didn't feel the urge to tell many people I was pregnant. We had now told the wider family, but I wasn't keen for it to be common knowledge beyond that.

The mother then proceeded to tell me that she, too, had suffered with morning sickness and felt so alone during the beginning of her pregnancy. Like me, she had chosen not to share her early pregnancy news.

Over the next few weeks, the pregnancy symptoms hit me hard. Sciatica, round ligament pain and heartburn, along with other aches from my changing body, all came raging through one after the other. The pregnancy sickness was unrelenting, and I felt like I'd been hit by a bus.

I'd signed up to a twins study, as I was happy to do my bit to help with research, but the main attraction was that it meant I got extra scans – a source of reassurance that I cherished as my brain continued to make me think the worst.

In the days and hours leading up to the scans I would be a bundle of nerves. Physically sweating while sitting in the waiting room, nervous that the sonographer would tell me that one or both of my babies had died. I would be temporarily reassured afterwards for a few hours, perhaps even a day, before the apprehension would come back with a vengeance. I wished there was a little window so I could peek at my two wriggly babies whenever I wanted.

Visiting the hospital where you work as a patient makes you see the service from an entirely different angle. I began to appreciate the frustration when appointments were running late. The nervous excitement as you waited to hear or see your baby. The apprehension while waiting to see the doctor. It really affected how I practised. I became more empathetic. I understood now that a midwife check-up might be the highlight of the week for a pregnant mum – a chance to see how the baby was doing.

One client who sticks in my memory from this time had, like me, a long route to pregnancy. Meera had been through multiple rounds of Clomid (a drug that stimulates ovulation) and many miscarriages. She appeared detached during the booking-in appointment but sat holding her husband's hand. Meera had been through this appointment more times than I could count on one hand across several pregnancies, and had still not managed to bring a baby home, so I could understand why she was reserved during the process. The reason this particular patient has stayed with me is because she was also pregnant with twins. I think I'm not alone in finding twins quite special and exciting. I felt happy for her, after all her years of waiting and heartache. I did not share my news with her but felt a kinship as we had both managed something so wonderful. I was full of optimism that after all her sadness she would be able to bring both these babies home this time.

Finding the right tone in the appointment felt difficult. From a professional level, I knew that there was little I could do that would change the outcome, other than my routine job and making sure she had all the correct referrals, pathways and help. My normal outlook was to assume that any patient I saw would be taking their baby home, and that my job was to try to facilitate that in a safe and supportive environment. Meera's experience was the exact opposite of this. Despite her having been pregnant many times, not one of those experiences had led to a living child. Therefore she could not share my optimism.

A few weeks later I came into work to begin an antenatal clinic. As always I would get to work an hour early so I could prep for my clinic and read the history of each patient. I saw that I was due to see Meera for her next midwife appointment and was looking forward to seeing how she was getting on. This would be the furthest she had progressed in a pregnancy. I clicked on her file on my computer and began to make notes on her history, so I was fully up to date before I was due to see her. This was when I discovered that, sadly, a couple of weeks after I had seen her, she had gone on to lose both babies. I felt heartbroken for her. There would be no opportunity for me to see Meera and let her know how sad and sorry for her I was.

Due to administrative failings, her appointment hadn't been cancelled. Far too often we are expecting patients to a clinic and they don't turn up. I always check on the system to see if a message has been left regarding the pregnancy, but more often than is acceptable there is simply nothing there. Instead, I call the patient to ascertain if they are running late, or have forgotten the appointment, only to be informed that they are no longer pregnant after experiencing a miscarriage. I can only imagine the hurt this causes – a reminder of how their pregnancy should be progressing, but sadly isn't anymore.

This news also caused a ripple of panic to flood through my body. I had an uneasy sense that my babies weren't safe. I found this difficult to balance as there was much excitement from friends and family about our news, which I could not share.

We had started house-hunting and had put our flat on the market. Viewing houses was taking every spare moment as we had decided to move out of London to Essex to be closer to my family. With two babies on the way, we figured we would need as much help as we could get. We would drive to see houses on our days off, knowing that these babies were likely to arrive early so time was not on our side. When looking at houses we had to factor in that we would have a life with twins. Could we fit two cots in the babies' room? Would the front door be big enough for a double buggy? Could the vendors move quickly, as we had no time to lose? We put offers in on a few houses, which fell through, but eventually we found a house that felt like it could be our home.

With an air-raid shelter in the garden, and lots of original features – fireplaces, picture rails, floorboards – I got that special feeling when I viewed it. I just hoped the babies would stay put until we were settled. The house needed some work – nothing structural, but this was not ideal if we had two newborns in the house. It wasn't really ideal if I was heavily pregnant either, but we would make do.

Time slowly ticked by. Most weeks I had some sort of appointment, whether that was a midwife appointment, an obstetrician appointment or a scan to keep me occupied, worried or relieved in equal measure. The obstetrician looking after me was a no-nonsense Greek doctor, who cared for all the patients who were expecting twins. In our first appointment she asked me whether I was planning a vaginal birth with these babies. She laughed when I said no, a caesarean would do just fine.

After the early scan had confirmed that there were two little babies in there, I'd decided that a vaginal birth would not be an option for me. Vaginal births of twins are not very common and it would be likely that one or both twins would be breech.* Although this didn't mean a vaginal birth would be impossible, vaginal breech births are not particularly common in the UK, and there aren't a large number of midwives who are experienced with this. As I was already feeling anxious about these babies making it into the world safely, a caesarean felt like the safest option for all three of us.

Before pregnancy, I had imagined that I would have a drug-free birth in a low-risk birthing centre. I wanted to experience labour, as I found it quite magical and I wanted to know what it felt like. I wanted to try to have as little intervention as possible, as I felt my body knew how to birth a baby. I can be quite stubborn and thought I would be able to bear the pain. I was keen to try hypnobirthing and imagined James supporting me through the labour.

I'll admit that I did feel disappointed that I would never get to experience labour, but I knew it was for the best. The obstetrician agreed and said I should aim for birth at thirty-seven weeks if all went well. She was also a foetal medicine expert and would scan me later on in the pregnancy. I felt safe knowing that she was looking after me.

Doing my postnatal visits and walking round London started to become more difficult, especially as I had a large, heavy rucksack filled with equipment. I wanted to try to stay as active as possible during the pregnancy, but I was amazed at how quickly my body was changing. My bump felt huge and very noticeable.

I developed significant round ligament pain, which was excruciating. It would suddenly flare up and would feel like I was being stabbed under my bump, in particular on the left side. I tried all sorts of exercises, cushions, lying in different positions, but it was so sore. I referred myself to our pregnancy physio at work as I was shocked at how much pain I was in so early in the pregnancy. It started

---

* Babies should ideally be head down for birth, but breech means they are bottom first.

at around sixteen weeks, and knowing I wasn't even halfway through I was worried for my mobility as the pregnancy went forwards.

James and I felt that signing up to antenatal classes wasn't something we were interested in. As I was a midwife, I didn't feel like it was something we needed to spend our money on. I always recommend them for first-time parents at work, but I wasn't sure I wanted to sit through the classes myself when I knew all the content already. I was keen that James learnt a bit more about parenting a newborn, but there was an online 'Dads-to-Be' class that I could sign him up to, run by my hospital. That being said, the unique challenge of parenting two babies at once did prompt me to see if there was any specific twins preparation we could do.

After some research, we found a twins antenatal course, which was run in a town near to where we would be living after the move. It was run by TAMBA, now known as the Twins Trust. We thought it would be good to pick up some tips about having twins, and to meet other twin parents.

When I went to book there was a list of terms and conditions, most of them to be expected, but one that jumped out at me was that there would be a full refund if your twins died. This made me feel uneasy, as it must have been something that happened fairly often if it was stated so clearly on the website. I tried to put this to the back of my mind and instead think about all the other twin-parents-to-be we might meet and make friends with. The course was to run in May, which would be in plenty of time even if the twins did arrive early.

I started to feel the babies kicking at around nineteen weeks. I had anterior placentas (this means the placentas were situated at the front of my womb), so I wasn't sure when I would start to feel them, as in that position the placenta can sometimes cushion the early movements. Their kicks were strong and would catch me unawares. James was with me the very first time it happened and could feel them in there. I couldn't tell who was who, but I knew there was lots going on in my uterus. Every kick brought a smile to my face. It made them seem even more real to me.

At around twenty weeks we were booked in for an anatomy scan, which is the routine scan when the structure of your baby is examined in detail. I had my usual scanxiety where I got myself worked up and came out in a sweat as I sat in the waiting room, worrying that one or both of the twins had died. This was almost normal for me, but once I had seen both heartbeats on the screen, I could relax and try to enjoy the moment.

For the first time, I went to the scan alone. James couldn't make it work around his shifts at the pub, so I went by myself. It was also with a different doctor who I had never met before, and she was all business and no chat. She performed the entire scan in near silence, occasionally pointing out a body part to me. At the end of the scan, she turned to me and said, 'Twin two has talipes,'* and pointed to the screen.

'Fixed talipes?' I asked.

I was told that the smaller twin had a club foot. The doctor then told me that my own consultant would rescan me in a week's time, and ushered me out of the room with a scan photo of the feet of my baby.

I called James and sobbed down the phone to him. I had an awful feeling that this was the start of everything going wrong in the pregnancy. It was so unexpected, as we had already had so many scans by this point and it had never been picked up previously. A part of me was also upset because the twins were identical, but this meant there would be a visual difference between them. I didn't want them to be different from each other. I worried this would mean the smaller twin would possibly be bullied.

I then phoned my mum and cried some more to her. I was of

---

* Talipes is the medical term for club foot.

course relieved to hear that there was nothing more sinister wrong, but it put me on edge. Having talipes is fairly common, affecting around 1 in 1,000 babies, and thankfully it is easily treatable. However, nobody wants to be told there is something wrong with their baby. I was no stranger to seeing unwell babies and the doctor couldn't rule out that there wasn't anything else affecting this twin, and it scared me.

We were due to be scanned by my consultant the next week, who would confirm the talipes, and then I would be referred to the paediatric department for a discussion about the treatment options that would be available post-birth.

A week later I was at home one evening and I noticed that I'd had some bleeding. It was bright red, but not a huge amount. My first instinct was annoyance. My blood group was A negative, and James' was A positive. Due to my negative blood group, any vaginal bleeding or significant knocks to the abdomen would require a visit to hospital for an injection of something called anti-D. This injection is a blood product, which would stop me from forming any antibodies if there was any mixing of mine and the babies' blood and they happened to have a positive blood group.

By coincedence James was off work too, so we drove to the hospital and were seen in maternity triage. I had phoned ahead and they were expecting me. As I walked through the doors and saw the friendly face of my colleague I burst into tears. I spluttered that I hated being pregnant, that it was so hard, that I was worried every single second of the day, that it was incredibly painful and I wasn't sure I could manage another sixteen weeks. After a hug and a breath, I calmed down and was ushered into a room to be checked over.

We listened to both the babies' heartbeats, and I had some blood taken. A doctor came and did a speculum to see if they could identify the cause of the bleeding. After looking, I was told I had a cervical ectropion. This is where the cells that usually grow inside the uterus are growing on the outside of the cervix. These cells are more sensitive than the usual cervical cells and more prone to bleeding or irritation. I had been told this before, so I wasn't surprised, and as it was harmless I was reassured that everything was well.

It was past midnight at this point, and waiting for the anti-D can sometimes take a few hours. I was due at a midwife appointment that day with my friend who had performed the booking-in appointment, and the anti-D can be given within seventy-two hours, so James and I decided to go home for a little bit of rest.

After a few hours' sleep, I was back at work, pounding the pavements of London, before heading into hospital. It was a Thursday. I had started to feel a bit under the weather by this point. I was still bleeding and didn't feel quite right, but just couldn't put my finger on what was wrong. I was still struggling with quite significant round ligament pain and overall wasn't feeling my best. As the round ligament pain had been so bad, I'd booked myself in with the physio and the appointment was this day. It was a class with other women. Most of them were in their third trimester, and mostly nearing the end of their pregnancies. I was only just halfway through mine and the physio seemed surprised to see me so early in the pregnancy.

The class didn't tell me much that I hadn't already tried, but we could put ourselves forward for one-on-one care from the physio. I signed myself up and left the class to go upstairs and have my midwife check-up. The anti-D was given (it really stings!), but I was still bleeding. It made me feel slightly uneasy, but I knew I had been checked the day before and my cervix was irritated.

It was quite a busy few days for me; I was due to be working over the weekend, and then on the Monday I was finishing my role as a community midwife, and instead heading into the hospital for a role in the Antenatal Clinic. This was because it was considered safer for my continuing pregnancy that I no longer carried out the postnatal visits carrying a heavy bag. It also meant I wouldn't have to do any shifts on call.

I'd also arranged for a friend to come over for dinner that evening. I really didn't feel up to it, but it wasn't like me to cancel. I hoped she wouldn't mind that I wasn't up for cooking. I hadn't actually told her I was pregnant, so that would also be a surprise. When she arrived she took one look at my growing waistline and it wasn't a secret anymore. We ordered a takeaway from a local place, and I could barely eat a single mouthful. I felt exhausted and I was desperate to go to bed. Once I was alone, I took Crumpet out for her nightly wee. By this point I could barely walk with discomfort but assumed I just needed a good night's sleep.

By the Friday morning I was feeling slightly better. James was off work, and we had planned to walk up to our local high street and get an ice cream as a treat. I was struggling to move, so we drove and popped into the parlour. We were seated at a table, but I couldn't sit. The pain, although bearable, meant that I had to perch or sway. I went to the bathroom, and saw that I was still bleeding, but it was thinner, almost watery. I was beginning to get really nervous. It had been three days now and I was still bleeding. I didn't want to bring it up in the middle of the café, so once we were home, and after a few more trips to the bathroom, I calmly told James that I thought my waters had broken.

We sat in silence on the car journey to the hospital. Through South-east London, then the South-west, over the bridge and north towards the hospital. I had phoned ahead again, and this time I was taken straight into a room. I showed the midwife my pad. She agreed: it looked like my waters had broken. I felt a bit numb at this point. I had so wished that I wasn't right.

We sat in further silence while the midwife called the doctor. To my surprise, my consultant appeared. She was covering the labour ward over the weekend. She scanned me and both babies were still there kicking around. She didn't think my waters had broken but wanted to do another speculum examination to check. While she performed the examination, James held my hand. I was sweating with nerves. At one point she looked up and asked me whether I'd had any children before. I was confused and shook my head. She confirmed that my waters had not broken, and I breathed a sigh of relief.

The next conversation was a blur. I was cannulated, bloods were taken, I was given thromboembolic stockings* and I was told I was being admitted. I'd packed an overnight bag before we left for the hospital, so this wasn't a surprise to me. After the consultant left the room, I asked to look in my notes to see what the consultant had written. I scanned down to the bit I was looking for. She had written: 'Cervical appearance: Multips os.'

The os is the opening of the cervix. Before you have had a baby your cervix is tightly shut, but once you have had a baby it never fully closes again. A multip is someone who has had a baby before. To translate, my cervix was beginning to open. This was not good news. I was twenty-one weeks pregnant – far too early for these babies to be born.

The guidelines in the UK specify that premature babies will be resuscitated if the pregnancy has reached twenty-four weeks or beyond – this is classified unkindly as the point of 'viability'. Some advanced neonatal units will consider intervening after twenty-three weeks, but at twenty-one weeks there was no such hope if these babies did decide to come early.

I was taken to a side room on the antenatal ward with its own bathroom. A small perk to being a staff member. James stayed with me while I unpacked, and until it was time for bed. I'd phoned my mum and kept her up to date. James was coming back before work, and my mum said she would visit me the next afternoon. I also texted

---

* These are tight stockings that aim to reduce the likelihood of developing deep vein thrombosis (DVT), which is a blood clot.

my team leader and told her that I wouldn't be able to work over the weekend. I felt dreadful letting the team down at such short notice, but there wasn't much I could do at this point. I needed to put my babies first.

I was exhausted, but I couldn't sleep. My side room was behind the nurses' station, so the lights were on and there was the gentle buzz of an antenatal ward. I drifted in and out of sleep, and I started to be woken up by an uncomfortable tightening in my stomach. It wasn't painful, but enough to wake me up. I was still having this bloody, watery loss, and so I was getting up every few hours to check and change my pad. I began to time the tightenings and noticed they were around every five to seven minutes.

Morning came, and the tightenings had settled down. I showered, dressed and nibbled on the corner of my toast. Then I sat and waited for James to visit. It was the weekend of the Oxford versus Cambridge boat race and as James' pub was on the River Thames, it was one of the busiest weekends of the year for them so he couldn't take the day off. It was not ideal that I was sitting in hospital, but I was hopeful that I would only be there for a few days.

During the morning ward round, my consultant came back to see me. My bloods showed that I might have an infection. I was started on a strong course of intravenous antibiotics, and more bloods were taken.

I tried to keep my spirits up. I had some visits from colleagues, which temporarily took my mind off worrying about my cervix. James left to go to work, and shortly afterwards my mum arrived. By this point the tightenings had started again. It felt like the waistband on my jeans was squeezing too tight, right at the pubic bone. I spent a while holding my waistband away from me in case it was that all along. The babies were both still wriggling around, which was comforting, but also uncomfortable, too.

I tried to eat some lunch but promptly vomited it back up,

along with the painkillers I'd taken. I attempted to take my mind off everything by starting a crossword, but then I started to feel exhausted, barely able to keep my eyes open. I tried to lie down on my side and rest, but the pain was getting worse and worse. I felt a strange sensation, and got up to go to the bathroom and check. Everything appeared to be fine, so I lay down again.

A few minutes later I felt a pop and a warm feeling spreading through my jeans. I jumped up and ran to the bathroom. I must have shouted out, because I heard my mum asking what was wrong. My trousers were halfway down my legs, and I'm not sure how I managed to get the words out.

'My waters have broken.'

The next thing I knew, Phoebe, the midwife looking after me on that shift, had come in. She was a young midwife, newly qualified, who I had known as a student. She left the room quickly to go and get one of the doctors. Almost immediately she came back with an obstetrician who I had known for a number of years, since he was a much more junior doctor.

My mum left the room and I told her to call James and tell him to come to the hospital. The doctor and Phoebe prepared to perform a speculum examination. I lay there, hoping and praying that this wasn't happening. That there had been a mistake.

There was no mistake.

This time my waters really had broken. My cervix was open. The doctor kindly said that I needed to be moved to the labour ward. Then my brain recognised what my body had been trying to do for the past few days. I was in labour. My babies were going to be born and they were going to die.

I turned to Phoebe and told her that I didn't want anyone to see me. The contractions were now frequent and painful, causing me to shout out every time I had one. I couldn't bear the thought of anyone, especially colleagues and friends, seeing me like this. I didn't want to look them in the eye as I was writhing in pain, knowing that I was on my way to watch my babies die.

If you have ever been to a labour ward, you'll know that they are busy places. There's constant hustle and bustle, with people at the desk, by the board, fetching things, going to theatre, making calls, cleaning, tidying and so on. They are full of activity and never quiet.

As I was wheeled out of my room and down the corridor to Room One – the bereavement room – the labour ward was a ghost town. Completely deserted. We did not see a single person. I had never in all my years seen it so quiet before. I was so very thankful to the entire team on that day who all stayed in their rooms so I could have some privacy in my worst moment.

James arrived as I was being wheeled into Room One. He had jumped in a taxi as soon as my mum had called. The contractions had really ramped up, and I was quite vocal. James came in to a noisy, slightly chaotic room, as Phoebe was trying to hand over to the midwife who would be taking over my care. James immediately burst into tears at seeing me crying and calling out, not fully understanding what was going on. He was shocked by how much pain I was in, how quickly everything had changed from the morning and how powerless he was to help me.

At some point I was handed the gas and air. Just as I had instructed many women to do over the years, as the contraction built I started to take long, deep breaths in on the gas. It didn't take the pain away, but it did give me something to focus on. The peak of each contraction was intense. Painful, but not unbearable.

I was asked if I wanted further pain relief. I thought about this only for a few seconds. If the pain wasn't there, I would have to sit and wait for my body to evict the most precious cargo it had ever carried. The thought of that was even worse than the pain that was rippling through my body. I knew the labour would be quick, as it often is with preterm labour, so I declined.

Water kept leaking from me, along with blood. I was kneeling on the bed, leaning over the backrest. Both babies were breech, and I knew this would be the best position I could labour in to help them come out. Despite being in labour and my world being turned upside down, I kept having midwifery thoughts on what should be happening or what I should be doing with unnerving clarity.

After no time at all, I felt something shift, and knew that the first twin was on its way. I turned to James and warned him.

'Don't be scared. They are going to look different, but don't be scared of them.'

These babies were too early and they would not look like chubby full-term babies. They would be red or pink, with fused eyelids and little body fat.

As I bore down, the eldest of our twins started to move downwards. The legs and body sort of fell out and I reached down and caught the baby in my hands. After a few pushes, the head was born. I looked down and brought the baby up towards me.

It was a boy.

We were having identical twin boys.

The umbilical cord was clamped and cut, severing our connection and any remote possibility of him staying alive. I held him close, while he gasped for breath. His tiny body working so hard to try to stay with me for as long as possible. He was slightly bigger than the palm of my hand. No hair, and bright-red translucent skin. The most beautiful lips with a perfect cupid's bow. Even his club foot was the most precious thing I'd ever seen. Ten perfectly formed fingers, and ten perfectly formed toes.

My heart swelled with pride and simultaneously broke into thousands of shards. We named him Cecil after my grandad. In this brief moment of calm James and I held him and each other. Through the tears we gazed at our baby in wonder that we had created something so precious and spent what little time we could adoring him.

Not too long afterwards my contractions started again and broke the peaceful moment as the second bag of waters burst. I knew it was time for my next son to be born. I passed Cecil to my mum, so she could hold him while James supported me through this next birth.

I felt the next baby moving down, and with minimal pushing his legs and body were born, too. He started cycling his legs, which is a classic movement associated with breech births. I was shocked that something so tiny would be doing all the normal things that a much bigger baby would do. Moments later, like his older brother, he was born into my hands. Another beautiful boy. Slightly bigger than Cecil, but just as perfect. He, too, had his cord clamped and cut before I could even process that this meant his oxygen supply would be cut off.

We hadn't fully decided on a name for this next twin, but in the moment we both knew that his name was Wilfred.

I spent some time cuddling them both, holding them close as all mothers do, drinking in every second of their lives, feeling the vast wells of maternal love swell up inside me almost in defiance of their fate. I was then pressed to try to deliver the placenta. Something which had slipped my mind until this point. After nearly an hour, the threat of going to theatre and a considerable amount of effort later, I finally birthed the placenta as well. A quick check to see if I needed any stitches, and we were left to spend time with our babies.

Mine and James' dads arrived shortly after and between us all, we cuddled and admired them while they both struggled with all their might to fill their tiny lungs with air. Like all new parents and grandparents, we looked for familial similarities in their faces, felt their breathing and expressed our love for them even in the most tragic of circumstances.

I tried to absorb every millimetre of them. Cecil's waters had been broken for two hours by the time he was born, so his poor face was a little swollen compared to his brother's, but that just made me love him even more. They were absolute perfection.

After ninety minutes of fighting as hard as they could, they both slipped peacefully away in our arms. Their short lives surrounded by love.

10

The Aftermath

The post-birth tea and toast that everyone usually savours tasted distinctly average. In fact, I'm not sure it tasted of anything at all. I vomited it all back up shortly after anyway. The post-birth shower was equally depressing. I wanted to be clean and to wash away the birth, but I was still quite faint from the birth and blood loss. James stood with me, and I'd never felt quite so embarrassed to be in front of him. Blood ran down my legs, and my stomach looked like a deflated balloon. There was nothing triumphant or joyful about this post-birth experience. No proud phone calls, no golden hour with skin to skin, no awkwardly passing the baby between us, worried about dropping or breaking them.

Instead, there was silence and disbelief. How had this happened? After all we had gone through to get pregnant, how could it all end so quickly?

We stayed in hospital for a few days. I was on IV antibiotics for a suspected infection and wasn't well enough to go home. Those days were a blessing. We spent our time eating sushi and cuddling our boys. It felt like we were suspended in time in the bereavement room. The world was still moving and turning outside of the room, but we were in a little bubble. We were protected. Our parents gently shared the news, so we were spared from making upsetting phone calls.

Getting to know our boys was a privilege. They had been dressed in tiny knitted gowns and hats. I had put these tiny outfits away in the store cupboard at work many times over the years. I had always said a little thank-you out loud to the grannies that I imagined knitting them. It used to warm my heart.

Cecil was shorter than his younger brother, so his gown covered his feet. Wilfred's feet poked out of the bottom of his gown, and I worried about them getting cold. When they weren't in my room, the boys were placed in a special fridge, so the reality was that they actually were cold. Perhaps it was my way of mothering them, trying to wrap them up and keep them warm like you would with a living baby.

During the pregnancy, I hadn't felt confident enough to buy any baby items. I would sometimes allow myself to look on the internet but would then quickly get worried about jinxing things and stop. I told myself I'd start buying things when I reached twenty-four weeks. This meant I had nothing to give Cecil and Wilfred after their birth. The guilt that rippled through me because of this was awful. I still feel it to this day. I imagined them feeling unwelcome because I hadn't prepared for them. No carefully chosen babygrow or blanket. Nothing to let them know how wanted they were. Instead, I kept them snuggly in a blanket knitted by James' mum, and two crocheted bunnies kept them company. I wished I had something to give them from us.

I became worried about them deteriorating, so it was a balance between having them with me and keeping them refrigerated. I wanted my memories of them to be as pristine as possible. Cold cots are available in many hospitals, which keep babies cool after they have died to try to delay some of the natural changes that occur. For some reason the cold cot wasn't offered and I didn't think to ask for it. Instead, they were placed together in a small Moses basket when they weren't being cuddled. I was more than confident when handling newborn babies, but our tiny boys seemed especially fragile. They could each fit in one hand. They were so beautiful to me, and I wanted them to stay that way for as long as possible.

Everything about them was perfect. Tiny fingernails, tiny eyelids, ears, toes. Everything was just as it should be but in miniature. They had my legs and the family cankles, James' shoulders and lips, my chin and hands. All their features were so defined, and being able to see the family resemblance was comforting. It was also bittersweet. Their eyelids were fused shut so we would never see their eyes. No hair had formed on their perfectly round heads, so we were left to speculate on their hair colour. We would never know what their smile looked like, how their laugh sounded, how their cry would sound.

When your baby dies, your body doesn't always get the memo. My body knew I had gone through birth, and therefore it was also going through all the normal postnatal processes. As this was all unexpected, I hadn't prepared. I didn't have any maternity pads. I hadn't stocked up on painkillers or bought breast pads. My freezer wasn't stocked with nourishing homemade meals. I hadn't even decided when I was going on maternity leave yet. I had thought about packing my hospital bag from around twenty-four weeks, as I was aware that twins could come early. I wasn't prepared for them to come this early, and I certainly wasn't expecting them to die. I had worried that if I had packed my bag too keenly then I would be jinxing it and something would go wrong. Not surprisingly, it turned out that the birth and death of my sons had absolutely nothing to do with whether I had packed a hospital bag or not.

* * *

I was swollen and sore, but my recovery from the birth seemed straightforward at first. I was up and about quickly. After my body had cruelly rejected my babies, it seemed keen to forget that it had ever been pregnant. The aches and pains that I had suffered were almost immediately gone. No more sickness, no more backache, no more sciatica or heartburn. No more babies either. No tiny little kicks in my tummy. I sometimes thought I could feel them still moving in there and would then heartbreakingly remember that they were gone. Phantom kicks, which felt comforting at first. Then grief would hit me all over again. My mind was unravelling and letting me down.

I'd been given a tablet to prevent any breastmilk coming in. I'd numbly taken this when it was presented to me without thinking. In hindsight this was a blessing. The thought of having swollen, leaking breasts as another reminder of what should have been would have seemed like an even greater insult. It was one less thing to worry about.

My consultant came to see me before we went home. She had been on call over the weekend, so was well aware of what had happened. I think she had known from the moment she performed my speculum examination a couple of days before that these babies were on their way to meet me. She said she was sorry. She looked me firmly in the eye and said, 'You will have a stitch next time.'* I nodded in agreement. She then asked if I had any questions. My mind was entirely blank, but my mum asked when I would be able to start IVF again. 'In six months,' she replied. I blinked. I wanted to start IVF again as soon as possible. Tomorrow if the clinic could fit us in. At this moment in time, I didn't want another baby, I just wanted Cecil and Wilfred, the babies I already had. Yet my arms were aching to hold a warm, living baby, and I knew IVF was our only option.

I was desperate. Desperately sad and desperately longing to be a mother to a living child. Six months felt like a lifetime. It was longer than I had been pregnant for. I knew that once the initial grief had

---

* A stitch placed through the cervix to try to keep it closed.

146

passed, my intense desire to mother would be exacerbated by this loss. I tried to comfort myself by thinking that perhaps I would be one of those people who fell pregnant naturally after having IVF. There was always hope. Surely, I deserved some good luck after this?

The stream of midwives and doctors coming into our room felt almost relentless. Routine checks of my blood pressure, heart rate, breathing rate and temperature. Drugs rounds with IV antibiotics. Catering staff with food that I had no appetite for. Midwives and doctors with paperwork. Consent forms for various procedures. The days whizzed by. We also had one very special visitor: Margaret.

When I was a student midwife we had a guest lecture from a charity called Remember My Baby. The charity funds photographers to come and take photos of babies who have died. It was an incredibly moving lecture. We were shown photographs that had been taken, and they were breathtaking. It was explained to us how the service worked, and how the charity came into fruition. Never did I imagine that I would be requesting my own visit from them.

Margaret came and photographed our babies with the most tender touch. She appreciated their beauty alongside us and provided us with some of our most precious memories. I didn't know how to pose in the photographs. Was I supposed to smile? Or look exactly as miserable as I felt? I didn't know the answer and had no energy to figure it out. Margaret made both James and I feel as relaxed as possible.

I hadn't even brought a hairbrush into hospital with me, and James had grabbed some clothes for me to wear. I wasn't looking photoshoot ready. Anti-embolism stockings and flip-flops weren't my strongest fashion look, but I didn't care. I was still hooked up to an IV line of antibiotics, which we tried to hide from the camera with carefully placed blankets and cushions. The shoot was short, then James and I were left alone with our boys again.

The hardest part about your baby dying is leaving the hospital.

When we said goodbye to Cecil and Wilfred we knew we would never see them again. Having to give them one final kiss goodbye, and then hand them back over to the midwife, was possibly the worst moment so far. The finality of it. I wasn't ready to say goodbye, and I wasn't sure I ever would be. We took the blanket they had been wrapped up in, and we left them with one of the bunnies that James' mum had crocheted, taking the other one with us. It went against every instinct to get up and leave. I knew that once we left, more paperwork would be completed and then the porter would be called to take them down to the lower-ground floor and into the mortuary. There they would remain until we had decided what our next plans for them were. The only solace I could find was that they were together and had each other.

We then packed up the few belongings we had taken into the hospital with us and left. James' parents had come to pick us up. They insisted on carrying our bags – a gesture of warmth and kindness. Over the past few days I had been to hell and back both physically and emotionally. I'm not sure I had the strength to carry any bags. This meant I walked out of those hospital doors empty-handed. My arms hung loosely by my sides, as I didn't know what else to do with them. No photograph of James holding two car seats. Instead, I held his hand as we made our way down to the car – partly to stop my legs giving way, and partly to feel connected to him.

We used my staff badge to exit through a staff-only door, so I didn't have to walk through the corridors and see the other parents leaving with their living, breathing babies. I wanted a swift exit where I didn't have to make eye contact with any colleagues. I felt ashamed. I didn't want my grief to be any more public than it needed to be.

The drive home from the hospital was grey and bleak. Dark clouds covered London's sky. The traffic moved slowly, and I simultaneously longed to be home and also dreaded it. I wasn't sure how I was expected to carry on with life. To go about our everyday activities when something so catastrophic had happened.

We went inside our flat and everything was how we had left it, before our world fell apart. It was like we had just popped out for a quick pint of milk from the supermarket. My pregnancy test was still on my bedside table, where it had sat for the past twenty-one weeks. My pregnancy pillow was still in the bed where I had left it, expecting to use it that night. The sight of it made me feel sick. I had hoped to use it as a breastfeeding pillow once the babies were here. I had bought it when my pelvic pain began. Now the pain was gone, but I would give anything for it to come back. I'd even take the sickness all over again if it meant I could still be pregnant with my boys.

* * *

The next day I woke up and squeezed my empty stomach into a pair of regular trousers. I had no need for maternity trousers anymore. I collected up the few pieces of maternity clothes that I had allowed myself to buy and hid them at the top of my wardrobe. I was no longer pregnant and didn't want the reminder that I should still be growing my two babies.

I then defrosted the freezer.

I needed to keep moving, and to keep my hands and my mind busy. Sitting still meant having to think and process what had happened. My brain was an odd combination of whirring thoughts and a void. I preferred the hollow setting; as long as I kept myself distracted, the pain wouldn't come.

My parents came round, and my mum and I set about doing the only thing we could to occupy ourselves: we cleaned.

Every square inch of our flat was washed, wiped and polished. I threw out bags and bags of our belongings. Nothing much felt important enough to keep. I recycled all the notes I had taken during my midwifery training. Pages and pages on how the reproductive system worked. How it changed to accommodate a growing baby within the uterus. I felt angry at my profession. How could this happen? How could my babies not be saved? With all the medicine available, with all the technology and inventions that saved lives, how was it that my babies couldn't be saved?

Every so often we would be interrupted by the doorbell ringing and I would go downstairs to receive another bunch of flowers from well-meaning relatives and friends. Sometimes I would feel moved by the gesture, and other times I wanted to scream and throw every single bunch of flowers in the bin. I was devastated, and flowers could not take away the pain of my babies dying. In my more rational moments, I knew that there was nothing anyone could do to make it better, and that the flowers were because other people were hurting for us, too. It was the way that people wanted to show they cared. I knew there was an outpouring of love coming our way, but still I yoyo-ed between feeling moved and feeling furious.

The emotions fuelled my cleaning frenzy. I stood at the top of a ladder, feeling faint with low blood pressure, my yellow Marigolds on, scrubbing my kitchen blinds. No one dared to tell me to stop, or if they did, I was deaf to them. What was the alternative? Sitting there crying? Tears rarely manifested themselves as I was too numb.

You walk out of hospital empty-handed with a deflated belly, and return to your usual life. Except nothing is the same. Your world has been blasted into smithereens, but the world still turns for everyone else. People go to work, come home, go about their daily activities, while you are suspended in grief.

There is very little follow-up or support after your babies have died. I wasn't offered any counselling. I had declined the option to have any follow-up care from the local community midwives. As I lived outside the catchment area for the community midwives from my hospital, I would be seen by a community midwife from a hospital more local to me, and I didn't want a stranger coming into my home and poking and prodding me. I didn't want to have to explain what had happened. I knew that half of the postnatal check would be missing – the check on the babies. Midwives are not trained counsellors or therapists, so apart from checking my blood pressure and asking how I was feeling, I wasn't sure what they were going to do for me. I wanted to keep my world small, and this meant pulling up the drawbridge and keeping people out.

I had been told to book a GP check-up for six weeks' time. Again, I knew this was a routine check-up, and would usually involve a check of the babies, too. Then I was told to await a debrief appointment in six to eight weeks' time. That was it. Otherwise, James and I were left to muddle through our new normal.

Along with deep-cleaning the house, I tried to get some life admin in order. James and I decided that we would go ahead with our house move. Although we had imagined our new house with two new babies in it, it felt right that we started a new chapter. I wanted to leave London and be closer to my family even without Cecil and Wilfred there. I couldn't go back to my old life. I couldn't pick up as if nothing had happened. There was plenty of house admin to keep us busy, which meant my brain could be busy, too. A fresh start would be good for both of us.

I also had the task of cancelling our twins' antenatal course. I thought back to the terms and conditions. It felt like it had been a foreshadowing that I had read how to cancel the course and obtain a full refund if the twins died. The money didn't matter, I just wanted my babies. I felt jealous of the other couples who would get to go on the course. They would all make friends with the other twin parents. They were going to bring home their twins. I was supposed to be a twin mother. I had done something so special by taking one embryo and making identical twins. The identical part felt particularly important. We might have needed IVF to conceive, but these babies were a miracle of nature. They were destined to be special. Instead,

I got a short but appropriately empathetic email response from the course, which cancelled our booking. I wondered if there would be another couple who would take our slot, or whether there would be an empty space where my growing bump should have been.

After two weeks James felt ready to return to work. I think he was keen to try to move away from all the sadness, to surround himself with people and talk his way through his grief. The flat felt oppressive with my mood, and he could keep himself busy with work. If I had thought the follow-ups for me were scarce, they were even worse for James. There was nothing other than a few leaflets for him. This was his loss, too. It might not have happened in his body, but he was grieving for two little boys just as I was.

I didn't know when I would return to work. My line manager had visited me in hospital and told me kindly to take all the time I needed. I had nodded without even thinking about how long that might be. I needed time to process all that had happened. It wasn't going to be easy, heading back in to work in the very same place where my babies had died. I put work to the back of my mind. The NHS would continue to function without me until I felt ready to return.

Crumpet, our dog, kept me occupied while James was at work. It meant I had to get up and walk her twice a day. If not for her, I'm sure I wouldn't have even bothered to get out of bed. I was conflicted in my attitude towards her. I disliked that I had to get up and care for her, while also being thankful for the company and for a reason to carry on. She had been a companion to me over the past few years when James worked in the evenings. When I fell pregnant, she had rested her head on my bump. As much as I loved her, at certain points I resented her. She was no replacement for my babies. She could not fill the space where Cecil and Wilfred were supposed to be. She would never love me the way a child loves their mother. I wanted to be needed the way a mother was needed. Yes, Crumpet needed me in a practical sense, but I craved the weight of a newborn in my arms. Walking her gave me a reason to get up and out, but I felt like I had to hide. I didn't go on my usual routes because I didn't want to see any of the people I knew and talked to on my dog walks. I kept to the woods and fields nearby instead of the park. I would walk for hours as I couldn't bear the thought of coming home to an empty flat. Once it was clean and tidy, and Crumpet had been walked, there was nothing for me to do but sit there.

Even the simplest of tasks felt difficult. From the outside, I looked like a normal person, but nothing about this new life felt normal. My sister took me out for lunch one day, and as we stood in the café ordering I just couldn't believe that so many people were going about their daily business. I felt like the death of my sons was indelibly etched on my skin. Could they not see that something completely catastrophic had happened? I felt angry that the world continued to turn, that people found things to laugh and smile about. Grief made me feel unwell. My eyes permanently hurt, I had a constant headache, I had to force my body to do tasks that should have come naturally – even walking required concentration.

A couple of weeks after the birth I noticed that it was slightly painful to sit down. As I hadn't needed any stitches post-birth, this confused me slightly. Surely things were supposed to get more comfortable, not less? Then, in the shower while washing I felt a lump on my vulva. It was sore to touch. The next day more lumps had appeared. The day after even more. I couldn't sit as it was so sore. I had no idea what was going on, so I booked a GP appointment. James drove and came in with me. The GP misunderstood and thought that I had living twins at home. When I explained, her face dropped and she stumbled over her words as she realised her mistake.

After taking a look, she reassured me that they were cysts, and that it was a response to being unwell and run down. I was relieved. My brain didn't seem to be able to think logically anymore, and it had raced through all sorts of awful possibilities. Perhaps I had cancer. Perhaps James had been having an affair and I had contracted a sexually transmitted infection. Maybe that was the reason I went into labour and Cecil and Wilfred died. Nothing seemed beyond the realm of possibility anymore. I felt humiliated that my body had not only let me down, but was also continuing to embarrass me. On top of that, my thoughts were incoherent, muddled and paranoid. Now that the worst had happened, it felt like more bad things would and could continue to happen.

After a few days of salt baths, the lumps were gone. I felt hideously unattractive at this point. The postnatal hair loss had started, and I was still bleeding and swollen. My dignity was in tatters.

Within three weeks of giving birth I went on a diet. Not a diet to lose weight; I went back on the fertility diet. As I'd eaten so poorly during pregnancy thanks to the morning sickness, I wanted to get back to some of my healthier habits. Life was feeling out of control, and this was my way of taking back some elements of power. When infertility was leading me into a downward spiral, cooking had helped me hang onto a tiny bit of my sense of self. Now, I might not be able to control my emotions, or the fact that my babies had died, but I could control what I cooked and ate. I dug out my fertility cookbooks and started ordering organic wholefoods for me to prepare. I baked oat cookies and bars, I boiled up bone broth to drink and I started taking all my supplements and vitamins again, including folic acid. Despite being heartbroken, I knew I still had a steep and probably long journey ahead of me towards holding a baby, and I had to start somewhere. My body felt like a stranger to me. It had betrayed me in the worst way possible. I needed to nourish it so it would be in the best condition, so I would eventually be able to hold a living baby in my arms. I wanted to be able to forgive my body for all I had put it through, and for how it had failed. I couldn't do that by abusing it. It needed kindness and understanding.

11

Birth and Death

'Viability'. My least favourite word in the dictionary.

In the UK, twenty-four weeks of pregnancy is known as the point of 'viability'. This means that if a baby is born after twenty-four weeks it will be offered intervention to try to save its life. If a baby is born before twenty-four weeks there is no legal responsibility for the medical profession to provide any life-saving support. In practice there is more of a grey area, as many high-level neonatal units will offer resuscitation from twenty-three weeks depending on the parents' wishes and the size and condition of the baby at birth.

Twenty-four weeks is the starting point for resuscitation in the UK because around this gestation, with the help of medical intervention, there is a chance that the baby will survive. Prior to this gestation there is thought to be very little hope that a baby would be able to survive with medical help. Even at twenty-four weeks, a baby may be able to survive, but the chances of it living with severe health problems are significant.

Viability limits vary around the world, but they seem to be around twenty-three to twenty-six weeks. This stage of very early prematurity is the most challenging time for a baby to be born.

I understood this well. It was my job to understand this. It's not something we discuss with parents, and I'm not sure why. I think because naturally we try to assume that each patient in front of us will carry their baby to full term. I'm sure parents would want to know in advance whether their baby has a chance of survival or not if it were to be born prematurely.

I remember the first time I saw a very early preterm birth. I was a student midwife, working with my mentor, Cathy. We were looking after Elaine, who was pregnant with her third child. She had been admitted onto the labour ward with threatened preterm labour – a phrase we use when we suspect that someone might go into labour, but labour has not started yet. Elaine was twenty-four weeks and two days pregnant. It was a night shift, and we had gone into the room to introduce ourselves and to perform some initial checks. We did basic observations on Elaine, we listened to her baby's heartbeat with a doppler* and we also checked the resuscitaire. This is an emergency device that is in every labour ward room. It is checked by the midwife at the start of every shift to make sure it has all the equipment it needs. When a baby is born needing some extra support we take the baby to this machine. It contains everything we need for dealing with a neonatal emergency, something that all midwives are trained in. Once happy with Elaine's vital signs, her baby and all the equipment, we left her to try to get some sleep.

An hour later, I opened the door and crept in to check on Elaine. She was asleep, and so was her partner, Thomas, next to her on the chair. No further checks were needed so I snuck out, trying not to wake her. Sleeping in a hospital is not easy. An hour later, she rang the call bell. I went in to see how I could help. She mentioned that she was beginning to feel uncomfortable and requested some painkillers. After Cathy brought her the painkillers I sat with her a while to see if I could notice a pattern to her pain, or if I could feel any contractions

---

* A hand-held machine that records the baby's heartbeat.

in her uterus. I couldn't feel anything and the pain settled. Elaine started to go back to sleep, so again I left the room. I relayed the interaction to my mentor, and I documented what had been going on in Elaine's notes.

A little later, the call bell rang again. This time Elaine was in significant pain. She had got off the bed and was standing next to it. I turned and opened the door, calling for Cathy to come and help me. I then turned and took the three steps from the door towards Elaine. I pulled a pair of gloves onto my hands and knelt beside Elaine on the floor, grabbing an incontinence sheet to put down in case her waters broke. I could see that she was bearing down. I lifted up her nightie to see if there were any external signs of labour. I heard Cathy enter the room behind me, and all of a sudden the amniotic fluid, the baby and the placenta all shot out onto the towel I was holding underneath her. I was so shocked that for a millisecond I froze. Then my instinct kicked in and I scooped up the baby and ran to the resuscitaire. Cathy had pulled the emergency bell and began working on the baby. I stepped aside knowing that as a student I had done all I was expected to do. An urgent neonatal call was put out, which called the crash team from the neonatal unit next door. Within seconds the entire room was full of midwives, doctors and neonatal nurses all working hard to save this baby. I went to check on Elaine. I reassured her that the doctors were doing all they could to try to save her tiny baby.

I had been so shocked at the speed at which this labour had progressed. Elaine had gone from relative comfort to delivering her baby in a matter of minutes. I had never seen a baby that small being born. On the resuscitaire the baby had been placed into a plastic bag to keep it warm. It was intubated to keep it breathing and various tubes and wires were attached to this tiny thing. Once the doctors had done the initial resus and stabilising,** they took the baby next

---

** Very premature babies will not be able to breathe on their own so will need help with this.

door to the neonatal unit. As the team wheeled the baby past the bed, they stopped so Elaine could get a glance. She had a daughter. Then the baby was gone.

I felt shaken by what had happened. I had not expected Elaine to give birth on our shift, or if she did begin to labour, I would never have expected it to be so extreme and fast. At this point in my studies I had seen babies go to NICU, but I had never seen a baby that small or fragile. I had seen countless babies be resuscitated. I was well versed in the emergency bell and the crash team, but this baby was different. I had held this baby, stopped it from dropping onto the floor. This was not the way I would ever want a baby to be welcomed into the world. I couldn't even really comprehend the wide range of emotions that Elaine must have been feeling. Knowing that your baby is clinging on to life and you are on the next ward, not being able to see or hold them. Once the baby had left, Cathy and I carried on caring for Elaine. We checked for any vaginal damage that might require stitches. We cleaned her, changed her bedsheets and brought her tea and toast. After a short rest, we then took her in a wheelchair to visit her baby in the neonatal unit.

A disappointing part of maternity care is that often mums whose babies have gone to NICU are expected to stay on the postnatal ward until their discharge. At my trust we had three side rooms on the postnatal ward. These would be offered to mothers who required special monitoring, or for mothers with babies in NICU. This meant they wouldn't have to be in the bay surrounded by other women and their babies. With only three rooms available, they would always be full, and sadly that meant that occasionally mums would have to spend a noisy night on an open ward with other babies crying. Knowing your own baby has been separated from you and is potentially extremely unwell in a neonatal unit, then having to fall asleep surrounded by other mothers cuddling, feeding and caring for their babies, must be harrowing.

One of the most upsetting parts of this particular case was that I didn't even get to find out what happened to the baby in the end. As a student midwife, I didn't have access to the computer system, so I couldn't look up the baby's records. Once Elaine was discharged from the postnatal ward the next day I had no further contact with her. I think about this baby girl and her mother often. I desperately hope they are at home together, after such a difficult start in life.

The twenty-four-week mark, or viability, is on the very cusp of life or death. Days do really make a huge difference to the outcome, and the longer you can sustain the pregnancy the better.

When my waters broke and my contractions started for real, I knew that at twenty-one weeks and one day, there was absolutely no way my babies would survive. Instead, I had to go through labour knowing that the very act of me giving birth would be their cause of death. No one had to explain to me that my babies were going to die. I knew that already.

In some ways, I am glad their short lives were spent being loved and cuddled by their mum, dad and grandparents. I'm not sure I would have wanted them to be subjected to tubes and needles only for them to die. But on the other hand, I just wish they could have been given a chance. Not at twenty-one weeks – I know that is too early. I wish my body had hung on for a few more days. Even thirteen more days, to make it to twenty-three weeks, which could have made the difference between death and a chance at life for them. Twenty days would have taken me right up to the threshold of viability, and they would have had the opportunity of life.

Many medical terms have little regard for the emotional impact they have. The word 'viability' can be used to indicate whether something is a workable option, or feasible. It feels so clinical – as if a spreadsheet has been drawn up, the matter has been considered, and Cecil and Wilfred were found to be lacking in some way, and therefore disregarded as a waste of time, energy and resources.

As a midwife I fully understand the reasons why their tiny bodies were not equipped for life outside of my body. As a mother, I feel strongly that Cecil and Wilfred were real people who I so desperately wish had had the chance of life. It pains me that nothing could be done. It goes against every instinct to simply sit by and watch them die.

The day after Cecil and Wilfred were born we were given various leaflets to help guide us through this challenging time. One of the leaflets explained that if your baby was born alive, regardless of the gestation, you would be entitled to a birth certificate. James was reading all the leaflets and pointed this out to me. It was a glimmer of comfort among the misery, that they would be recognised and known to the world. This is something I was aware of through work, and yet in the moment it was like I was learning it for the first time.

It felt so reassuring to us to know that there would be official documentation of our boys' short lives. The next time the midwife came into the room to chat to us, James mentioned the leaflet and asked how we would be able to obtain the birth and death certificates. The midwife shook her head. She explained that our babies were born too early to have birth and death certificates. We showed her the leaflets and again she shook her head, stating that the leaflets were wrong. We were confused, but also not in the right state of mind to argue, so we took her word for it.

Over the next few days and weeks at home I kept reading that babies born alive, regardless of the gestation, should be entitled to a birth and death certificate. I couldn't understand why all the literature I was reading said this, but we had been told the complete opposite at the hospital. My mind felt so muddled and I wasn't sure what to do.

Six weeks after the birth we attended the hospital for a debrief. The aim of the appointment is to spend time with a specialist doctor understanding what happened and making a plan for any future pregnancies. The doctor in question had not been involved in my care, but I knew her from my time working at the hospital. My experience of working with her was that Dr Desai was a particularly compassionate doctor.

She had looked through all my notes and discussed why she thought I might have gone into labour. At the time it had been assumed that I might have an infection. My inflammation markers had been raised, but there had been no convincing signs of infection.

I asked whether she thought my cervix might have been the issue. Dr Desai shrugged and said it was difficult to say. She recommended that I had my cervix measured in a future pregnancy. I mentioned that my original consultant had recommended a stitch in my cervix. Dr Desai wasn't convinced by this, and I wasn't convinced by her lack of commitment. I knew she couldn't say for certain what the issue was, but I wasn't going to be happy with a 'watch and wait' approach. I was going to push for a stitch in any future pregnancy.

At the end of the appointment, Dr Desai asked if we had any feedback. I mentioned that the leaflets we had been given had been misleading as although the twins were born alive, we weren't able to get a birth certificate for them.

Dr Desai stared at us.

'The twins were born alive?'

James and I nodded, confused. Surely this was all in our notes?

Dr Desai shook her head. There had been absolutely no mention that Cecil and Wilfred had been alive post-birth in the notes. She explained that we had been right all along: if they were born alive then we would be able to obtain birth and death certificates for them. She apologised profusely and said she would look into this. Our appointment ended and James and I left the room, not sure what to think.

It took us about an hour to get home. Shortly afterwards, my phone rang. It was the bereavement midwife from the hospital calling. She was responsible for overseeing the care for bereavement cases, although she had not been present at our sons' birth. As soon as I answered the phone she began to apologise. She'd had no idea that the twins were born alive.

It was at this point that I completely lost it.

I felt absolute rage, and I shouted down the phone to my colleague. It felt like I was losing Cecil and Wilfred all over again. They had lived for ninety minutes each. How on earth had this happened? Not only were my sons dead, but my own colleagues had somehow managed to wrongly record them as stillbirths.

James and I had been so proud of how hard Cecil and Wilfred had fought to stay alive. I felt it was a huge part of their story. We wanted that bit of paper that said yes, although they died, they also lived.

After a few weeks, and several meetings, emails and phone calls later, we still didn't have our birth and death certificates. The midwives who attended the birth claimed they never saw Cecil and Wilfred alive. James and I were floored. We had sat and commented on how amazing it was that they were alive. My mum had commented on it. In fact, James' dad, who had arrived around an hour after the birth, was also there in time to see Wilfred living for a short while.

We saw them agonal gasping. This is the body's last-ditch attempt at drawing air into the lungs. As Cecil's and Wilfred's lungs were so immature their attempts were not successful, but their tiny bodies were trying so hard to suck air in. Wilfred had been kicking his legs while being born, again something we had all commented on.

But no, the midwives were saying they never saw them alive.

I couldn't believe it. One of the midwives attending the birth was an experienced midwife who I'd looked up to. I had known her for close to ten years. I had learnt a lot from her during my time as a maternity support worker, a student midwife and now finally a midwife.

It appeared it was our word against theirs.

The only thing I know is that they didn't actually look at the boys after their birth. Cecil was born, and after a few minutes I passed him to my mum while I laboured again. The focus was on my second labour. Then, after Wilfred was born, the placenta took nearly an hour to come and there was considerable effort involved. This meant, to my knowledge, that they never actually looked properly at my boys. I also think that, because the outcome was always going to be death, perhaps they didn't think it was important to look for signs of life.

But it was important. It was so important to me. Knowing that my boys tried with everything they had to live means the world to both James and me.

They are so many reasons why not being able to have a birth and death certificate hurts me. One of the reasons is that there is no official record of them. Their legacy only continues if we keep talking about them, keeping them alive in our hearts, despite the continued grief in remembering their loss. In a generation's time, their existence is erased. There is no official record of pregnancy loss before twenty-four weeks. They aren't on any official registers, so it will be as if they never existed. Nothing breaks my heart more than this.

I have no reason to make up that they were living. I certainly wasn't imagining it. Four different people saw them alive. Myself, James, my mum and James' dad. Two of those people were midwives – myself and my mum. We weren't distraught with grief; we were calm and comforted by their attempts at life.

After twenty-four weeks, regardless of whether your baby was born alive and subsequently died, or whether your baby was stillborn, you are required to register both the birth and death. This also means that you are entitled to maternity leave and maternity pay. Before twenty-four weeks your baby must be born alive to entitle you to any maternity leave or pay.

As my babies were wrongly registered as stillbirths and were below the twenty-four weeks gestation there was no maternity leave for me. I was not entitled to anything. I was not seen as a mother, despite giving birth to two babies. Technically I was required to go back to work the following day. Some countries do provide pregnancy loss or miscarriage leave, but in the UK there is no legal leave following a loss of a baby at less than twenty-four weeks, so in order to take time away from work many people use their sick leave. I wasn't sick, though. I was recovering from pregnancy and birth. I was grieving.

The maternity pay didn't matter to me. I couldn't have cared less about the money at this time. It was about the principle. I could have taken the time to grieve and process what had happened properly. It was also about the recognition that I had been pregnant and given birth to two beautiful babies.

As I'd been told not to worry about work and to come back when I felt ready, I felt well supported by my employer. I couldn't even look ahead to the end of the day without feeling overwhelmed, let alone think about when I would return to work. I put it to the back of my mind and assumed I would know when I felt ready. Or I would be asked to return. Either way, it was for future Sophie to worry about.

* * *

We never did end up with birth or death certificates for our babies. I researched online and found other people who had contested a wrong stillbirth notification. It would require a long and expensive legal battle on our part. A battle with no guarantee of the outcome we wanted, and had we failed it would have felt like losing Cecil and Wilfred all over again.

I couldn't juggle (or afford) going through the courts while also undergoing IVF, and if I was lucky enough to go through another pregnancy, I knew I needed to give all my attention to that. I would have fought with every ounce of strength I had, but I knew I also needed to use all my reserves, both emotional and financial, to bring home a living baby. For this, I felt immense guilt – choosing a future with a baby I had no guarantee I would ever have, over the two boys I had carried, loved and held.

12

A Final Farewell

Having to plan a funeral for your children is something that no parent should ever have to do. I didn't know anyone who had lost a baby before so had no one to ask how you go about arranging a service. My brief experience at work had been explaining to families their options, but no more than that.

We decided that Cecil and Wilfred were very real people to us, and that meant that they needed their own funeral and day to be celebrated. It ended up being a very positive experience, and yes, it was tinged with sadness, but I'm proud of how we honoured the lives of our sons.

Many funeral directors will arrange services for babies at no cost. This wasn't something I was aware of previously, having never had to think about it before. There is a government initiative called the Children's Funeral Fund, which in England goes towards the cost of a funeral for a child. I think this goes to show just how awful it is to have to say goodbye to a child, regardless of their age or gestation.

James and I decided we didn't want a postmortem on Cecil and Wilfred. We had the placenta sent off to histology,* but I wanted Cecil

---

* Histology is the microscopic analysis of biological tissues.

and Wilfred to be left alone. I knew they were completely perfect, and there wouldn't be anything to come back from the report. This is a very personal decision, and for some families having a postmortem will absolutely be the right thing for them to do. For us, the reason Cecil and Wilfred died was because they were born very prematurely. I knew that already, and having a postmortem wouldn't give me any more information that I didn't already know. This meant that their bodies could be released from the hospital as soon as we were ready.

Families who decide to have a postmortem will have to sign various consent forms to agree that this will happen to their baby. Then, once they leave the hospital, the baby goes down to the mortuary, and from there it is arranged for the baby to undergo the postmortem. For many hospitals, this does not happen on site. Instead, the baby will be taken to another hospital where a specialist will undertake the procedure. Once this is completed, the baby will then usually be returned to the original hospital, and from there the parents are informed and can make the arrangements for a funeral to take place.

The report from the postmortem takes longer, as there may be tests sent off during the procedure. These will need to be processed and analysed before the final report is put together. On average it takes around six weeks for the final report to be completed. Parents will then have a specialist appointment to go through any findings once the report is available.

The hospital provided us with some information on what could happen with Cecil's and Wilfred's bodies. Many hospitals perform group ceremonies at regular intervals, where several babies will be remembered. We decided this wasn't for us, and instead wanted to arrange a private funeral with Cecil and Wilfred being cremated.

A few days after the birth, my mum got in touch with a funeral director local to her and a week or so later they came round to my parents' house to discuss arrangements with us. We spoke about what we wanted for the service and were reassured that anything important would be taken care of by them without us needing to worry. There was a local celebrant who was an acquaintance and so we decided they would perform the service. James and I are not religious, so we just wanted a small celebration of their lives at the local crematorium. This was the crematorium that my grandad had been cremated at, so it already had some positive associations for me.

Due to the crematorium being particularly busy at the time, it would be five weeks before the funeral could be held. I'd have liked it to be earlier, as I wanted to get it out of the way. That sounds cruel, but it was such a difficult time. The funeral felt like it required a lot of emotional energy, so I wanted to dive straight in and get it over and done with so I didn't have it hanging over me.

We had to arrange the practical things. James and I signed forms to consent to Cecil and Wilfred being released from the hospital for the funeral director to collect them. The funeral director assured us that they would take good care of our boys, and I believed them. I felt comforted knowing that they would be respected and well looked after.

One day after they had arrived in Essex, I drove to sit outside the funeral home. It was located on a road I had driven down hundreds of times, and several times since Cecil and Wilfred had been taken there. In this instance I felt an overwhelming urge to be near to them. We were given the option to visit them, but we both agreed that we didn't want to. We had said our final goodbyes to them when we left the hospital. I didn't want to have to say goodbye to them all over again. I also didn't want to see them in case they had deteriorated significantly. I wanted to remember them as the tiny, perfect little boys they were. Sitting outside and knowing I was near them was enough. I hoped they knew that I hadn't abandoned them, and that they were so loved.

As we were keeping the funeral small, there wasn't too much

to organise. We chose a coffin for them to be in together. I looked through two or three books of coffins and didn't like any of them. Nearly all the coffins we were shown for babies had frills or bows or were incredibly fussy. I just wanted something plain and simple. In the end, I found a small wicker coffin, which seemed just right for them. It was plain, without anything adorning it. Flicking through a brochure full of coffins is a surreal experience, and not one I wish to repeat in a hurry. I was choosing something I didn't want, for an event I didn't want to arrange, for two people I desperately loved but hardly knew.

The thing with arranging a funeral for a baby is that you don't know them. That's the devastating part of baby loss. A whole life has been stopped before it even started. There are limited memories or experiences. When a baby dies, they are so incredibly loved, but the sad thing is that you never got to know who they really are. I have been left wondering who those two tiny babies could have become. The limited memories we have are of them inside my stomach, growing and kicking each other. The few glances we got of them during the scans. The ninety minutes that they lived for, and the couple of days we spent with them after their birth and death.

James and I didn't want a hearse or a procession. We wanted to keep it low key and understated. There would only be James and myself, along with our parents and siblings, attending. We asked for the coffin to already be in position when we arrived at the crematorium. We did discuss whether James wanted to carry the coffin down the aisle to the plinth. He didn't. He wanted the last time he held them to be when they were in his arms in a blanket being cuddled, not in a coffin. He was also worried he might not physically be able to do it. Not because of the weight of the coffin, but because of the weight of the grief and responsibility.

A week or so later, the celebrant came round to my parents' house so James and I could discuss what we wanted from the service. This celebrant had lost a child himself many years ago, which, although sad to hear, was also comforting in a way. He had been where we were. He knew that we were living out our worst nightmares. Many years had gone by since his daughter had died, and he told us that he had gone on to have a happy and fulfilling life. He had two other daughters who gave him plenty to smile about. He told us that it had drawn him and his wife together in a way that, unless you have experienced loss, you can't quite understand. I hoped that James and I would be similar and find an even stronger bond through this challenging experience. I couldn't imagine anyone ever understanding the way I was feeling quite like James did. We had held each other up during the past couple of years. 'For better, for worse' had never seemed more apt.

After some discussion we chose two poems and agreed that we would go away and pick three songs to be played during the ceremony. James also decided that he wanted to write and give a eulogy. I toyed with doing a reading but knew I wouldn't be able to maintain any semblance of calm while standing in front of everyone. I was in awe that James was going to put himself through something so emotional.

My mum arranged the flowers, which were beautiful. I wanted one small posy to sit on top of the coffin, and then some smaller flowers to decorate the outside. We had referred to Cecil and Wilfred as 'the peas' during the pregnancy, as the two of them were together in their pod. I'm sure many people expecting identical twins do the same. For this reason we chose sweet peas in the bouquet along with some roses and daisies. The colour palate was greens, yellows and whites. I didn't want lots of blue as I'd never really bought into the 'blue for boys and pink for girls' style. Neutral and understated was the atmosphere I wanted.

Choosing the music for the funeral was one of the hardest parts. I find music quite emotional, and over the years I'd found myself listening to less and less in a bid to stop myself getting caught up in my emotions. This was because anything even vaguely soppy would reduce me to tears and anything that was upbeat would crowd my brain. The only way I can describe it is that my brain was so busy and loud with all the thoughts of infertility and pregnancy that I couldn't take any more noise from the outside. James was the opposite. He sought solace in music.

* * *

The day of the funeral arrived. It was one of those days that I both wanted to be over, but also didn't want to have to go through with. I hoped it would feel like a bit of closure, but at the same time I knew it was moving us further away from Cecil and Wilfred.

We had spent the night before at my parents' house, so we would be close by rather than driving from London in the morning. Deciding what to wear had been hard. Although I was mostly back to my pre-pregnancy size, I felt my body wasn't quite the same. I hadn't wanted to buy a new outfit as I couldn't face shopping. I managed to find a navy-and-white dress in my wardrobe that fitted. James wore a navy jacket, with a shirt and trousers.

We drove the short distance to the crematorium and waited outside with my parents and brother and sister. The sun was shining and it was pleasantly warm. The service was at ten o'clock in the morning. As we waited outside, I looked through the window into the room and saw a tiny coffin right at the end. It took my breath away. It was so very small. The funeral directors had put a teddy bear next to the coffin, which took me by surprise. It hit home that this was a funeral for two babies. I had only been to a couple of funerals previously, all for adults who had died at good ages, having lived long and fulfilling lives. I never expected to attend a funeral for a baby, and never in my worst nightmares did I think I would have to attend one for my own children.

As we stood outside, we looked at the order of service. Here we could see the list of funerals that were taking place that day. It was a list of names – from memory I think it was around eight. Ours was the second on the list.

Baby Cecil Martin and Baby Wilfred Martin.

Seeing their names like this amplified that we were doing something out of the ordinary. I wondered if any other visitors to the crematorium that day would look at the list and see their names. I wondered whether they would be shocked or saddened by this. I wondered if they would mention how cruel it was that babies could die. Whether they would notice the fact that they were twins and remark that this was special or doubly heartbreaking.

James' parents and his brother and girlfriend all arrived, and at ten o'clock we all walked to the front of the hall. We sat in two rows; the rest of the room was empty. Our celebrant was professional, welcoming and friendly, and did a wonderful job of leading the service. Despite us taking up such a small amount of space, it felt personal and intimate.

When the time came, James stood up and delivered a breathtakingly moving speech. A touching demonstration of his love for our sons and our family. I'm beyond proud of him for showing such poise and being such a wonderful father to our boys. Having the strength to show his vulnerability and emotions has always been one of the traits I love most about him, and I hope he passes that down to our children.

Following the service we walked outside and stood chatting in the sunshine. Once out of the building I breathed a sigh of relief. It was over. My brother gave me a big hug and for the first time that day, I felt tears well up in my eyes. I choked them down. I didn't have any energy left and I worried that if I started crying, I wouldn't be able to stop.

There was a small area for each of the funerals that day to receive flowers. I hadn't wanted any flowers so Cecil and Wilfred's area was empty. I felt guilty. I wondered if other people at the crematorium that day would notice the empty space where the flowers should be.

Infertility had made me feel like I didn't fit in for the past couple of years. And even here, on the day of my sons' funeral, I still felt like the odd one out. We were the parents cremating their babies. Funerals were supposed to be for old people who had lived long and happy lives, not for people whose lives hadn't even begun.

We collected the posy from the top of the coffin for me to keep. Later on, I pressed the flowers in glass frames, and they are hanging in my bedroom.

The day felt surreal. I was going through the motions – none of it was sinking in. It almost felt like it was happening to someone else, and I was outside of my body, watching.

The day had been exactly what we'd wanted so far. Beautiful weather, and all our closest family by our side. I felt lucky to have such supportive people surrounding us. It wasn't just our loss. Our parents had both lost two grandsons, our siblings had lost two nephews. Everyone had been so excited about having identical twins in the family. They were so wanted and loved by everyone.

We had arranged to go out for lunch, and as the service had been so early there was some time to pass. Once we were finished at the crematorium we drove back to my parents' house for a cup of tea. The hard part of the day was over. We then drove to a pub in a nearby fishing village for lunch. The sun shone as we walked along the seafront. Everyone was chatting and the atmosphere was upbeat despite the circumstances. I couldn't help but wish we were out with a double buggy. I hoped none of the waiting staff were going to ask if we were celebrating something, and fortunately it didn't come up.

It had been a good day. It was the day I never wanted, but I know that James and I organised a commemoration that was full of love for two very special boys.

13

Salt in the Wound

Following the funeral lunch, we drove back my parents' house to pack up our belongings and drive back to London. Before we left, I went to the bathroom and it was as if all of a sudden my brain started working again. It had been so fuzzy for the past five weeks, but now the funeral had passed things were clear again. It was in the bathroom with my newfound vision that I realised I was bleeding heavily. In fact, I'd been bleeding heavily for the past five weeks.

As a midwife, I knew that post-birth you could bleed for around six weeks. When working in the community we discharge most of our patients by two weeks, and many of them will have stopped bleeding by then or will be experiencing a light bleed or even brown discharge. I knew these things could vary from person to person, so I hadn't been overly concerned. I'll also admit to not really thinking about it.

I changed my pad and then got in the car so James could drive us home. The journey took an hour. I went to the bathroom when we got home and saw that I had drenched my pad. I changed it and waited to see how long it would take to fill again. Ninety minutes later the pad was soaked. I looked back over the past few weeks and at one point the bleeding had looked like it might stop. I couldn't remember how long ago that was, but I had certainly been bleeding heavily for a while at this point.

I told James that I thought there was a problem. He looked at me, not quite sure how serious the problem was. I could feel myself beginning to panic. During my training we had been taught about various emergency situations, and one symptom that is sometimes mentioned is an impending sense of doom. This is the only way I can explain how I was beginning to feel. I told James that if I went to bed that night, I was going to bleed to death and not wake up in the morning.

I then began second-guessing myself. I was frightened of going to A&E in case I was laughed at. I wondered whether I should know better because I was a midwife. I questioned whether this was grief talking. I knew I needed medical attention, but I also didn't want to be seen as the sad woman with dead babies who was overreacting about normal post-partum bleeding.

After going backwards and forwards on the course of action, and knowing deep down that I needed to go to A&E, I decided not to listen to myself and instead called 111. I explained to the call handler that I was bleeding heavily and was changing my pad every ninety minutes. After some further questions, she informed me that she needed to speak to her senior and would call me back.

Some two hours later, when James and I had been sitting on the sofa trying to stay awake, we received a call back saying I should go to A&E straight away. They did offer to send an ambulance, but I declined. I still felt like I might be overreacting, and an ambulance definitely seemed like too much.

I packed a hospital bag, and we repeated the drive to the hospital. Through South-east London, then the South-west, then over the bridge and north towards the hospital. The last time we had driven here it wasn't good news, and I had a feeling it was going to be the same all over again. By this point it was late in the evening, around 11 p.m. James dropped me off outside, and went to find a parking space. I made my way to the A&E reception and repeated the story to the receptionist. I missed out the part about my babies dying. It didn't seem worth the effort to explain.

James walked in and we had barely sat down before being called in to see the triage nurse. I explained again that I was bleeding heavily five weeks from giving birth. Yet again I failed to mention that my sons had died. I knew that if the nurse looked me up on the computer system, my medical records would pop up and say it all. I'd also brought my discharge summary with me, which mentioned that Cecil and Wilfred had died.

After being shown back into the waiting area, we again had barely sat down before we were called into Majors.* I almost laughed. I should have trusted my instinct all along instead of sitting and waiting on the sofa for someone to give me permission to go to hospital.

The on-call gynae doctor was called and came to see me. He said he was sorry to hear about my miscarriage. I blinked. 'Miscarriage? I didn't have a miscarriage. I gave birth five weeks ago,' I heard myself saying.

My vital signs were reassuringly all normal. After some poking and prodding of my abdomen, I was sent home and told to return to hospital for a scan at 11 a.m.

We got home at around two in the morning and got into bed. I still wasn't sure whether I would wake in the morning, but I was so exhausted by this point that I succumbed to sleep.

I got myself dressed and headed into the hospital the next day. James was meeting his cousin for a coffee and a heart to heart before going on to work. As the hospital appointment had been so last minute he didn't have much time to rearrange and I thought it would

---

* Majors is an area of A&E for patients requiring urgent medical attention, as opposed to Minors, which would be for non-critical injuries, such as small fractures or wounds requiring stitches.

do him good to have someone to talk to, which meant I was going to attend the appointment by myself. I promised I would call him as soon as I had been seen with an update. I walked myself down to the train station and made my way to my work. Looking back, I can't believe I got public transport alone when I was bleeding so heavily, but it made sense at the time. I planned on popping in to see my manager after the appointment to discuss my return to work, now that the funeral had taken place.

My scan was taking place in the early pregnancy unit (EPU) as this ward also housed the rapid-access gynae service. I was very far from being in early pregnancy, but there was nowhere else to be seen. I made my way up to the fourth floor and waited.

When I had first started working at my trust, the EPU was situated on the third floor with the rest of the maternity services. Thanks to some ill-thought-through logic, the entrance was also the same as for the birthing centre. This meant that coming through the same set of double doors were women in labour and women miscarrying. Even if you didn't bump (excuse the pun) into a labouring woman as you entered the EPU, often you could hear someone in labour. Imagine being told that your baby had no heartbeat, and then having to walk out into the rest of the maternity unit.

It is likely that whoever designed the wards initially thought it was useful to have all the maternity services together. It makes sense; all the obstetricians and gynaecologists on the same floor, making it quick and easy to get about. Little to no thought was given, though, to the lived experiences of women who were having early pregnancy complications. Mine was not the only trust designed this way. I have heard from countless women who have received bad news, only to then have to walk through what felt like a tide of pregnant women.

Thankfully, during some ward renovations, the EPU was moved to the fourth floor away from the rest of the maternity services. This allows patients who attend this department some privacy as they navigate early pregnancy complications. As midwives we had limited interaction with this ward. We would make referrals, or direct women to this service if they were experiencing early pregnancy bleeding, but I rarely went up there, or if I did, it was never in the best of circumstances.

My appointment at the EPU was supposed to be at 11a.m., but I arrived a little early, as I couldn't let myself be late. The waiting room was small, with only eight seats, so I took one in the corner by myself. Two couples were there, too. I sat and waited – and waited. I could see that the department was busy. I overheard the nurses at the desk talking about an ectopic pregnancy. I knew this would take priority at it is a gynaecological emergency.

I waited some more. Both the couples were taken into scanning rooms and came out smiling and laughing, clutching scan photos. I knew that not everyone was in this ward for happy reasons, and that for many of them there must be a great deal of worry and stress, but even so I felt devastated. They had a pregnancy ahead of them. They were growing a baby inside of them, whereas I was soaking through pads in the EPU after my babies had died.

After over an hour of waiting, I was called in to be scanned by one of the consultants, Dr Chambers. I didn't know her particularly well, but we had worked together a few times. Dr Chambers said she was sorry to hear that Cecil and Wilfred had died, and then proceeded to take a medical history from me, asking me lots of questions about my symptoms. She then asked me to undress from the waist down for yet another internal scan and called in a nurse to chaperone.

I lay on the couch while she scanned the inside of my uterus. I stared at the ceiling as my insides were prodded. I began to count the tiles on the ceiling to distract myself. They were all grey, with a large light in the middle of the ceiling. It had been turned off, so the screen on the scanning machine would be more visible. I wondered what I had done to deserve this.

After a few minutes, Dr Chambers related her findings. It turned out there was a 2.5cm piece of placenta still hanging around inside me.

I was furious. How was this happening to me? Tears began to stream down my face as I realised that there was more upset to come. It made me so sad. My body still thought it needed the placenta. It knew it should have been in there for another fifteen weeks or so and didn't want to give it up.

The doctor went on to explain that I had two options. I could wait for the piece of placenta to pass by itself, or I could have surgery to remove it. I had already waited five weeks, this piece didn't seem to be able to find the exit, and my desperation for this nightmare to be over meant that I didn't want to wait a moment longer, so I opted to have surgery to remove the piece. The doctor went through the risks and booked the surgery for the next available slot. I was told I would receive a phone call with the details, and then I left.

As I walked out of the room, more couples were sitting in the waiting room, hoping to see their babies. I left with a swollen and puffy face from crying. My babies were dead, and I needed surgery to remove the placenta.

I walked to the lift and rummaged around in my bag to find my phone. It was half past one, and I had been in the EPU for over two hours. I had twelve missed calls from James and several messages. The last message said that he was worried that he hadn't heard from me and was coming to the hospital to try to find me. He was walking into the main reception as I made it down to the ground floor.

Relief flooded his face when he saw me, followed by concern as he saw that I'd been crying.

'I thought something terrible had happened and you had been rushed into surgery, as I couldn't get hold of you.'

I promptly burst into tears again and told him that something terrible HAD happened, and that I was going to need an operation.

James called his pub and arranged cover so he could come home and be with me. I was immensely thankful. I then called my mum and sobbed as I told her the story. If I wasn't so sad about it all, I think I would have laughed. How was it possible that this was happening? Surely, I had been through enough already?

Once I had composed myself, we walked to the Antenatal Clinic, where I had been due to start work the week after giving birth to Cecil and Wilfred. I explained to my manager what was happening, and that I would be staying off work until the issue was resolved. She was kind and supportive, and told me there was no rush to return.

I had been thinking about going back to work, as I was getting bored at home. Bored of the sadness. Bored of trying to fill my day when I felt so empty. My life felt out of control and I desperately wanted some normality again. Not that anything would ever be normal again, but I thought going back to work might give me a purpose. Once the placenta issue was sorted, I would think about returning to work again.

I contacted my acupuncturist to see if there was anything she could do to help the piece of placenta vacate the home it was finding too cosy. She kindly agreed to see me the next day. She reminded me of the aromatherapy oil clary sage. I could have kicked myself – why hadn't I thought of that myself?

Shortly before I qualified as a midwife, I did a short course in pregnancy and labour aromatherapy. Clary sage is a powerful essential oil, which can be used to bring about contractions. I started sniffing it at every opportunity, hoping I might not need to have the surgery.

A few days later I got a call telling me to come to the hospital the following week. No other details were given other than the date, time and location given to me over the telephone. I hadn't been given any leaflets about the operation itself, or what to expect from the day, and I was so exhausted I didn't think to ask. I put my trust in my colleagues, hoping that they would take good care of me.

I packed a bag, expecting to be in as a day case. James drove me to hospital again. The route brought up memories of our recent drives to the hospital, all ending in bad news. The nervous silence in the car. The worry of what was in store for us this time.

I made my way to the Treatment Centre on the ground floor. I checked in and waited in the reception area while James parked the car. It was here that I saw signs everywhere saying that no visitors were allowed into the Treatment Centre. As I hadn't received any details in advance, I hadn't realised that once I was called through, I wouldn't see James again until my discharge.

My heart sank. I was about to have an operation that I didn't want, following the death of my babies. I really wanted him to be there to hold my hand; it would have made such a difference. A nurse came and called my name. James squeezed my hand, kissed me goodbye and then went to find somewhere to wait. I choked back tears.

The Treatment Centre was divided into two separate areas; one for men and one for women. The nurse took me through and showed me to a changing room. She instructed me to undress and put a gown on, explaining several times that I needed to take my underwear off as I was having a gynae operation. After she had finished her spiel – clearly something she repeated several times a day – I had to explain that I was still bleeding heavily and would need to wear some underwear so I could wear a pad. She bustled out to find me some disposable underwear and then left.

Once changed, I was instructed to sit in the female-only waiting area. I had brought a book with me, but I was in no mood to read. Instead, I stared at the front cover while tears streamed down my face.

I watched the hustle and bustle of the unit. Doctors, nurses, anaesthetists, porters, healthcare assistants all rushing round. I saw a doctor colleague and he smiled. I arranged my face into something that I thought was neutral. I watched as they decided on the order of the list for that day. Being a staff member has some perks, and I was selected to go first.

The anaesthetist came to see me and was incredibly friendly, but I couldn't match his enthusiasm. I was cannulated and bloods were taken. I had already mentioned to several staff members that I was going to need anti-D following the procedure as my blood group was negative. This was a precautionary measure due to the nature of the procedure, as each potential exposure to foetal blood could lead to antibodies being formed. I knew this wasn't something that would be routine practice for them here in the Treatment Centre and could take time to arrange.

The operation I was having was an ERPC – an evacuation of retained products of conception. This is also the procedure performed when a patient opts to have surgical management of a miscarriage. I knew full well that everyone that day would glance at my notes and assume I'd had a first-trimester miscarriage. Only Dr Chambers, who had seen my notes in the EPU, would know the full story. It wasn't that I wanted to talk about it, just that I wanted a level of understanding that I was going through something quite unique and very painful.

Although I was first on the theatre list, the day seemed to take a while to get going. I was sitting in the shared female waiting room with about six other women of varying ages. I couldn't help the tears from falling, and I tried my hardest to cry discreetly. I didn't want to draw any attention to myself. I felt so alone despite being in a room full of people. I wished I could have a small amount of privacy, so my grief didn't have to be so exposed.

Eventually I was walked round to the theatre. I sat on the bed while the team ran through checks. I confirmed my name, date of birth and the procedure I was here for. I lay looking at the ceiling. It was painted. Stars and planets decorated the tiles above me. My chest heaved as I lay there crying. I closed my eyes and pictured my sons as the drugs were injected into my veins and I drifted off into a medicated slumber.

* * *

I was still crying when I awoke a short while later.

'My ... babies ... died.' The drugs had made my emotions all bubble to the surface and pour out to the nurse looking after me. Hilda was her name. She was older, in her sixties. Bobbed grey hair, with wrinkled hands, pink cheeks and a kind face. She was Scandinavian; I could tell from her accent.

She checked all my vital signs and then fetched me a glass of water. I managed to calm myself and take a sip. I didn't have any pain, just an uncomfortable feeling, as if someone had been rummaging around in my insides. Which they had.

Once I was well enough my belongings were brought to me, and I was told to change back into my regular clothes. I shifted my bottom to the edge of the bed, then put my feet on the floor. All my limbs appeared to be working, so I stood up. I had been sitting on an incontinence pad and it was covered in blood. I immediately panicked, imagining a worst-case scenario where my uterus had been punctured and I was going to bleed to death.

In the months when we experienced infertility and then went through IVF I had noticed that my ability to be rational was diminished. When life seems to be throwing hurdles your way, you start to expect hardships. Since Cecil and Wilfred had died, this had been exacerbated. When the absolute worst happens, you start to imagine that the worst will always happen.

So despite me knowing that bleeding post-surgery was normal and the blood loss was not excessive, I felt so traumatised by the sight of blood that I froze for a moment, worrying that I was going to die and wouldn't be able to say goodbye to James.

After a few deep breaths, I managed to persuade myself that there was no active bleeding and got myself dressed. Before I was moved, I asked Hilda about my anti-D injection. She assured me that it had been ordered and that in the next recovery area the nurses would administer it to me.

I was taken to a final room. This was mixed male and female, and we were seated in big armchairs – the wipe-clean NHS kind that recline. Hilda handed me over to a different team of nurses. There were so many in this area that I didn't catch anyone's name. People were coming and going. Doctors were coming to review patients. It was loud and busy.

An hour or so later Dr Chambers came to see me. She said it had been a difficult operation, and she had tried her best. She hoped it was successful, but we would have to wait and see. I sincerely hoped that was the end of it all.

I waited seven hours for my anti-D injection, despite being clear from the moment I was admitted that I was going to need it. When it finally came, it stung so much that I cried all over again. I was the last patient in the Treatment Centre, and they must have felt so sorry for me that eventually they let James come in to be with me. Just having him there made everything better. We managed to crack little jokes and make each other smile despite the misery of it all. Eventually we made it home.

The next day I woke up and decided it was time to go back to work.

14

Incompetent Cervix and Other Niceties

That day, I called my manager and asked if I could return to work. I felt I'd had enough of the sadness. If I went back to work then perhaps I would feel more like my old self again. As I had no entitlement to maternity leave, I knew I was on borrowed time. Although my managers had all been so generous in stating that I could take as much time as I needed, I knew the NHS was chronically understaffed and I felt guilty for not being with my team.

Staring at the four walls of our flat while wishing the past six weeks hadn't happened wasn't doing me any favours. We agreed I could start back the following week. My brief time off had been seven weeks in total. Not the maternity leave I had imagined. No coffee dates with friends, no baby classes, no endless piles of dirty baby clothes to wash, no pram-pushing in the park, no pacing the flat desperately trying to rock a baby to sleep. Plenty of sleepless nights, but for all the wrong reasons. The only nappy changes I was doing were the giant maternity pads I was wearing thanks to the ongoing bleeding. Post-partum hair loss didn't miss me out either. I was more than ready for a change.

On the Monday, I arrived at work early, as always. I can't be on time, let alone late; I have to be early or I start panicking. I made my way to the changing room and started getting changed into my tunic. It fitted perfectly and I felt that familiar pang of sadness as I did up the poppers over my stomach, which was no longer rounded. A colleague and friend came in, and I quickly pulled myself together. I couldn't start crying before I'd even got changed. We started chatting.

'I was so sorry to hear about your boys.'

I breathed a sigh of relief. I was so worried that everyone would be too nervous to bring it up, and it would be one of those awkward unsaid issues. I hoped people wouldn't worry about upsetting me. In fact, all of my colleagues said something to me about how sad and sorry they were. I knew they meant it, and it made the whole day easier. There was already the required number of staff on the ward, so there was no pressure for me to stay working if I felt overwhelmed.

As I had previously been working in the community and not at the Antenatal Clinic, it felt like a fresh start. I observed my colleagues running their clinics for a few days, getting to grips with small practical details about the place. By the end of the week I was back running my own clinics, and it felt like such a relief. Deep down I knew that I would never be the same person that I was before, but I wanted so much to experience normality. This was the closest thing.

I felt like a complete failure as a woman. As a person. But one thing I knew I could be good at was being a midwife. I loved my job, and had done so from the first moment I stepped into the hospital. I still wanted to be the best midwife I could be, and I didn't want to sit around feeling sorry for myself anymore. I wanted to make sure other women and their babies were safe and supported. I wanted to know I was making a difference to the lives of others.

I had to try to figure out how to navigate my new reality as a mother without her babies. Now, when patients asked me whether I had children, I wasn't sure what to say. I wanted to stay true to my boys, as the thought of pretending they didn't exist broke my heart. At the same time, I didn't want to scare any of my patients and I didn't necessarily want to go through all the details.

I worried that patients would be upset hearing my story, which would be equally distressing for me. Maybe they wouldn't want me as their midwife. How could I be trusted to look after anyone else's baby when I hadn't managed to look after my own? Of course, no one ever said that, but it was one of my fears.

I tried to remember all the patients I had looked after who had been through adversity, hoping that I, too, could make it through this bumpy road and end up with a living baby in my arms. Like Jean, who a few years before had appeared in the phlebotomy room doorway one day asking for a blood test. As our clinic was located within the gynae department, I wrongly assumed she was in the incorrect department. I asked whether it was for a pregnancy blood test. She replied that it was. I was confused. Jean looked older than my mother. Was the blood test for her? I waited to see if she was going to call her daughter in from the doorway. Instead, she confirmed it was for her. I invited her into the room and ushered her into the chair and took her pregnancy folder for a quick look. Jean was in her fifties, and desperately wanted a baby, and had decided to go it alone. The courage it must have taken for her to go through the process alone was impressive, with the stigma of her age against her – let alone the physical toll it would take on her.

I was very used to seeing women in their forties. It was routine, and a large majority of our overall patients were in this age bracket, so I wouldn't bat an eyelid. This was something quite different, though. I was intrigued and wanted to know more. Which IVF clinic had treated her? Had she faced lots of prejudice?

She had gone abroad to Europe for her treatment after she couldn't find a clinic willing to treat her in the UK. She had used donor eggs and donor sperm as she was single. This was a much-wanted baby, with a complicated story. The blood test was over quickly, and so I waved Jean goodbye and wished her luck.

Jean turned out to be a regular at our clinic, as due to her age she had appointments most weeks, either for a scan, or with the doctor or midwife. Having that many appointments meant she was such a familiar face around the department that by the time she came to giving birth she had a whole team of cheerleaders behind her. Her planned caesarean was uncomplicated and a few days later she was home with her son to start their life together. If she could get there, so could I.

While I threw myself into work like never before, the bleeding continued. It had lessened, but it was still going. I was regularly nipping up to the EPU for scans, swabs and blood tests. It looked like the piece of placenta was still there. There was talk of a further operation to try to clear it. This didn't fill me with joy, but I was certain that this ongoing saga needed to end so I could start IVF again as soon as possible.

The operation was booked, and a few days before the bleeding appeared to have stopped. I walked the three flights of stairs up to the EPU for a quick scan. I stared at the ceiling while I sat with my legs in stirrups and once more had an internal scan. It was gone. I had passed the piece of placenta. I couldn't quite believe it. Eleven weeks after my body had cruelly expelled my sons but decided to hold on to this last piece of placenta, it was finally over.

I felt myself walking back down the stairs with a spring in my step. On my lunchbreak I called my IVF clinic and booked the next available appointment. I couldn't help myself.

It wasn't that I had already moved on from Cecil's and Wilfred's deaths. Far from it. I was devastated. I just needed to hold a living, breathing baby in my arms as soon as possible. I knew that it could still be months or even years before I saw a positive pregnancy test again, so the sooner we got the ball rolling, the better.

My IVF clinic managed to fit me in the following week, but this time with a different doctor. In fact, this was a doctor I had previously worked with at my hospital and I was relieved. Having a familiar face there, and someone who is rooting for you, makes a huge difference to the experience of your care.

When the day of the appointment came, James and I hopped on the train and made our way to the clinic. Sitting in the waiting room brought up lots of emotions. I should have been at home with my infant sons, exhausted from sleepless nights and changing nappies over and over. It felt like I was further away from a baby than ever.

Dr Mali was appropriately empathetic and set about making a plan for us. We still had one embryo frozen from our first cycle. This had matured a day later than Cecil and Wilfred's embryo and had been kept in the freezer. We could have used this one, but I wanted to do another egg collection. If we were to have more than one baby, we would need more than one embryo. The younger I was when we collected the eggs, the more likely it would be that they would turn into embryos. This meant leaving that embryo in the freezer and pushing forward with more stimulation of my ovaries.

We discussed the drugs regime, and Dr Mali felt that it would be in my best interests to do a much shorter protocol this time to try to recruit as many follicles, and hopefully eggs, as possible. I had been very worried about scarring to my uterus following the retained placenta and the suspected infections, so we agreed to a HyCoSy scan* before starting IVF on my next period. When the day of the HyCoSy arrived, I was nervous. No pain relief would be provided, and I wasn't sure how painful it would be. I sat once more in the waiting room, trying to distract myself with a book. As always, I would be looking round trying to figure out what brought people to the clinic. There really was no walk of life that hadn't been in this waiting room. People of all ages, races, sexualities trying to grow their

---

* HyCoSy stands for hysterosalpingo contrast sonography. It is a type of scan where fluid is pushed into the uterus and fallopian tubes to check for damage.

families. More often than not I would be the youngest person there, which was both reassuring and not reassuring. I wondered what they thought of me sitting there.

Once in the treatment room, I undressed from the waist down and lay on the couch. A different doctor, who I had never seen before and never saw again, came in to perform the procedure. It was over in a few moments, and throughout all I could feel was warm liquid trickling down my bottom as it leaked out of me.

At the end of the scan, the doctor assured me that everything was normal. She handed me a report and then left. I dressed and left the room clutching my report, then left the clinic and headed for a nearby bus stop, which would take me to work. As I waited, I read the report in full. It said the structure of my womb was normal, and everything inside the womb looked normal. Then in a small font right at the bottom of the page it said my cervix looked normal, followed by the statement that the cervical length was 21mm.

My stomach dropped. I thanked my lucky stars I was a midwife and knew what was actually 'normal' or not: 21mm was in no way a normal length for a cervix. It is usually 30 to 40mm long, and is considered too short if it is less than 25mm. It was in that moment that I knew why Cecil and Wilfred had died.

I had an incompetent cervix.

I had never given that phrase much thought before. I had, of course, looked after women who had gone into premature labour. I had also looked after women with cervical stitches, which is one of the treatments for an incompetent cervix. Still, it wasn't a phrase I had ever used, nor one that was often in my vocabulary.

The cervix is the neck of the womb. It stays closed during pregnancy to keep the baby growing safe inside the womb. As the woman comes close to her due date, her cervix begins to change in readiness for labour. Once labour begins, the cervix shortens and opens, allowing the baby to pass out of the uterus into the birth canal. With an incompetent cervix, the cervix opens much too early, often in the second trimester. This can be for many reasons, such as undergoing surgery to the cervix or sustaining trauma to it from a previous caesarean. It could also be genetic, or because of a structural abnormality within the womb. Sometimes, as in my case, there is no known reason why it happens.

It is sometimes also known as a weak cervix or cervical insufficiency; terms which are both just as delightful. I know it can be incredibly upsetting for someone to hear these terms being applied to them. It can bring up feelings of shame, inadequacy and guilt. The consequence of this condition can be the premature birth of your baby, which, as with mine, may lead to their death, or a stay in the neonatal unit with a very unwell baby, which is also incredibly distressing. Hearing that a part of your body is incompetent is emotive, and even more so when the health, and sometimes life and death, of your baby is the outcome.

Unfortunately, the labels applied to women are vastly different from those given to men. A man may experience 'premature ejaculation', but a woman does not have 'premature cervical opening'; she has an incompetent cervix. A man may have 'erectile dysfunction', but a woman does not have 'cervical dysfunction'; she has an incompetent cervix. These small differences apportion the blame to the person, rather than accepting that a body part is not functioning to its fullest. The word 'dysfunction' simply means something isn't working properly. It has very few connotations of a person being inadequate or at fault in some way. Whereas 'incompetent' is a word that is sometimes used to describe a whole person. Someone can be incompetent at their job. It can be used as an insult. As if it wasn't bad enough that your body isn't working in the way it is supposed to, using language that puts the blame on you for something that is out of your control only exacerbates the situation and is unnecessary.

Language matters, especially in healthcare. It affects how patients perceive their conditions and situations, and can have a profound impact on their self-esteem. A person is more than their component parts or their medical condition. When they are made to feel judged or blamed for their health condition, it seems to me that they are less likely to engage with the service. Whereas feeling supported means they are more likely to take positive steps to help themselves as well as engage with the service provided.

When I am feeling particularly angry at myself, I think the phrase 'incompetent cervix' is entirely fitting. It let me down in the worst possible way. Yet, I wouldn't want anyone else calling me or my cervix that. Looking at it more generally, it seems that gynaecology and obstetrics in particular have a history of using blame-filled language: 'inhospitable womb', 'irritable uterus', 'failure to progress', 'failed induction', 'poor responder' – the list of terms that suggest the blame for any sort of deviation from the normal lies with the woman could go on and on. Even the word 'miscarriage' implies a woman 'miss-carried' her baby. She did it wrong, and that is why her pregnancy ended and her baby died. A 'late miscarriage' implies the woman forgot to miscarry on time. These terms fail to separate the medical condition from the whole person. They are loaded with negative connotations in an already emotional situation. Medicine isn't here to judge, it is here to treat, and to do so with respect, dignity and compassion, and the language used ought to reflect that – especially within maternity, gynaecology and obstetrics, where we are dealing with so much more than a body part. The ability to safely and successfully bring a child into the world is hugely emotive, even without uncaring language thrown into the mix. Language is a uniquely human thing and therefore we have to use it humanely, too.

It is possible to use neutral terminology, which simply states the facts of the medical condition without any negative connotations. Sadly, change within the medical profession can be slow, and there is much still to be done, but gradual changes are occurring. One example is the term 'geriatric mother' – historically used to describe a mother who was over the age of thirty-five. Thankfully this is no longer in use, and hopefully the other phrases mentioned above will also fade away.

* * *

Following the discovery that my cervix was abnormally short, I sat on the bus and did the only thing I knew I could do: I made a plan. Without a plan, I would feel paralysed and overwhelmed. When things felt out of my control, coming up with various options was one of the things that kept me sane. I emailed a doctor colleague, Dr Smith, who specialised in treating short cervixes, explaining what had happened to me.

At lunch we met up and Dr Smith stated that I needed a cervical stitch. To be precise, he suggested a transabdominal cerclage (TAC). I knew of this stitch because he was one of the few consultants in the country who inserted them. This meant that we saw more of them going through our hospital than many other hospitals did. The TAC is a permanent stitch that is inserted through the abdomen. The incision is made along the same line as the caesarean scar, and a strong, permanent stitch is placed high on the cervix. Unlike vaginal stitches, which are removed before birth, this stitch stays in forever and means the only option for giving birth is a caesarean. It is the most reliable stitch available but not often recommended due to how invasive it is, and because of the inability to have a vaginal birth afterwards.

Sign me up. I knew I wouldn't be happy with a vaginal stitch, knowing that something stronger was available. I didn't care that I wouldn't be able to have a vaginal birth anymore. All I wanted was to know I had done everything in my power to make sure any future babies stayed safe inside me. Dr Smith explained that I needed my

GP to do a referral, and then I would be added to the waiting list. I was so thankful that I was a midwife and knew that this option existed. The report from the IVF clinic made no reference to my cervix being abnormal, and the doctor was happy for me to start IVF again straight away. Without my clinical knowledge, I could have potentially got pregnant too soon and risked going into premature labour all over again.

While I waited for the surgery date to come through, I often thought back to Michaela, who was the first patient I ever saw with a TAC. I was working on the antenatal ward, and she had been admitted due to some vaginal bleeding. She was a complex patient. Aged forty, this was her first pregnancy: an IVF conception, which had followed a long fertility journey. There had also been some operations to her cervix, which had led to her having the TAC inserted. She had developed obstetric cholestasis (a liver condition) during the pregnancy, too. She spent several weeks on the antenatal ward where I looked after her. The plan was to try to get her pregnancy as close to thirty-six weeks as possible.

I felt for her. The monotony of people disturbing you with ward rounds, blood-pressure checks, drugs rounds, the lunch trolley and so on meant that the antenatal ward was far from an ideal place to convalesce. Both day and night are noisy on the antenatal ward: inductions coming and going, women admitted for early labour breathing loudly to manage their contractions, cardiotocography (CTG) machines beeping away – there is never a quiet moment. And if there is, everyone knows never to mention it, or before long the ward will be heaving again.

The days chugged past and eventually the day of Michaela's caesarean came. A good-sized baby girl made it earthside, much to everyone's relief. I knew the months of wondering whether this stitch was going to keep her baby safe inside her were not easy, but it reassured me thinking back to her and remembering all she had endured to bring her baby home.

After a few phone calls to the secretary, the date for my surgery was booked. In the meantime, we had moved out of London and back to my home county of Essex, to the house and home we expected to bring our boys back to. I closed the door to the room we had earmarked as their nursery. One day, I promised myself, I would sit in that room feeding my baby to sleep. But until then I tried to focus on the positives of being close to my family. I needed the support of having them nearby.

On the morning of my operation, I got up and left the house just after 5 a.m. James had to work, and I wanted him to come and visit me once I was out of recovery, so I made my way there alone. When I got to the hospital, I headed up to the fifth floor to the surgical theatres. Working as a midwife meant I didn't really venture outside of the maternity department much, so this was out of my comfort zone.

Gowned and waiting, I was asked by one of the nurses if I would do a pregnancy test prior to the operation. I balked, knowing it would be a miracle if two lines stared back at me. Still, I dutifully took the pot and filled it – half praying it would be positive, half praying it would be negative so I could go ahead with the op.

A little while later I was walked round to the anaesthetic room. I took this to mean the test was negative and my op was going ahead. The team cannulated me, and then the anaesthetist kindly gave me a spinal injection.* This was because the operation is known to be painful, and when I woke up I would be pain-free.

I had seen hundreds and hundreds of spinals and epidurals, but that didn't mean I was relaxed about having one. There was something about the idea of having a needle in my back that sent a shiver down my spine. I shouldn't have worried, because the consultant anaesthetist was such a whizz that it was over before I even realised.

---

* An injection into the back, which numbs you from the waist down.

Then I was laid on my back, and before I knew it, I was being put to sleep.

* * *

On waking, I was greeted by Hilda, the nurse who had looked after me when I went to have the placenta removed. No tears from me this time. Just the realisation that I now had a scar that looked exactly like a caesarean wound, but with no baby to show for it. I remember lying on the bed and lifting up my gown to inspect my wound. As it was covered with a dressing, I couldn't see it, but I was still terrified. Had I just undergone major surgery for no reason? What if I never got pregnant again? Unlike a caesarean scar, which could be a reminder of a baby being born, my scar was a reminder that my body had failed me and my children had died. On the other hand, I hoped that scar would one day be the reason that my future babies stayed alive. That I, too, could look fondly down and be reminded of a birth where I got to bring my baby home.

Once we got home, James helped me back into bed and I lay there feeling so incredibly thankful that the stitch was in place. The following week we took a trip to Norfolk to recharge and prepare ourselves for the upcoming marathon we were about to undertake. We were finally able to embark on IVF again, seven months after Cecil and Wilfred had died.

15

Trying Again

I'd frequently heard that if I stopped trying for a baby, I would miraculously fall pregnant. It was laughable, really. How could I stop trying, when all I could think about was having a baby? I was never not trying. Even when I didn't track my cycles every time we had sex, I would beg my body to cooperate.

During pregnancy I'd felt too unwell to even think about sex. Morning sickness coupled with pelvic pain was not a recipe for romance. On top of that, I was scared. Despite having counselled countless women that sex during pregnancy was safe, I couldn't bring myself to try it.

Sex post-birth means having to rediscover your body all over again and how to share it with someone else. For many people it's also juggling the exhaustion of a newborn, alongside actually finding the time.

But sex post-baby loss is a whole different ball game. Not only are you learning about your new post-birth body, but there is a huge emotional hangover from the grief. For those of us whose body has contributed to the loss, the guilt and blame can of course affect self-esteem. I was still hating my body for letting me down. I couldn't love myself at this moment in time, and couldn't see how James would be able to love me and my body either. Eleven weeks of retained placenta and bleeding had also meant that the recovery process was much longer than I had anticipated.

At the same time, I wanted to reconnect with James.

We had drawn inwards and found solace in one another. Remaining connected was a priority for me, but I was nervous. My vagina, which had previously been associated firstly with pleasure, had become less and less private.

I felt like my vagina wasn't my own anymore. Countless dates with Wanda, the ultrasound probe, meant that I felt like I'd lost ownership of something that was supposed to be mine. I was required to share that part of me with people whose name I sometimes didn't even know.

Then I'd got pregnant and had to push out two tiny humans bum first, against my will. This was followed up by the many weeks of bleeding, and far too many people rooting around trying to remove that stubborn piece of placenta. My vagina suddenly had a history that I hadn't anticipated. I felt disconnected from it.

When we did start having sex again, I couldn't stop myself from thinking about how Cecil and Wilfred had been born. I would recall the sensations I felt during labour and birth. Not in an unpleasant way, but more like a form of muscle memory. My body was remembering what had happened there before. How it felt when I knew the birth was imminent. A heaviness I could feel. I found it hard to switch off these thoughts. In a way it was a relief that we would be going ahead with IVF, so there was less pressure on having sex to conceive.

I was finding work particularly emotional at this time. Not only was I feeling my own complicated set of post-loss emotions, but I would be deeply affected by what I was seeing at work. Things now stayed with me in a way they didn't before.

I would be upset thinking about certain patients for a long time after I saw them. For example, Grace had been booked in for an elective caesarean. She was terrified of sustaining any vaginal trauma from birth – a very real fear, and something that no one could guarantee wouldn't happen. The day after her caesarean had been booked in the system, her baby girl decided that she couldn't wait any longer and contractions started coming at thirty-six weeks – three weeks before the operation was due.

Grace and her partner, Dave, arrived at the unit with bags in tow, not sure what to expect. Grace was assessed and not quite in established labour, but this baby was likely to be born the same day. The team discussed with her the pros and cons of the modes of delivery, but Grace was committed to a caesarean. Unfortunately, the ward activity that day meant that as Grace's baby was happy and safe inside, other patients whose babies were compromised took priority. Several hours had passed and by the time Grace was moved to theatre and almost ready for her surgery, she began to bear down and it became obvious that this baby couldn't wait any longer.

No doubt thanks to the bright lights in theatre, Grace's oxytocin levels must have taken a nosedive because her contractions promptly stopped (oxytocin is the hormone that causes contractions). We waited for them to start up again, but oxytocin is a shy hormone. It was not the warm, cosy environment that the body needs to feel safe enough to have a baby. Eventually her uterus got going again and some contractions started to build. Some dark hair could be seen on her baby's head. More and more hair, as the head moved forwards and backwards up the birth canal.

Grace bore down with all her might, and with a little help from a ventouse cup, her daughter was born. She was a good size for thirty-six weeks, but quite shocked from the delivery. A nice rub with a towel and she pinked up nicely but was still a little floppy. I kept rubbing her, while blood from the cord continued to supply her oxygen. When it became clear that the little girl needed a bit more help, the cord was clamped and cut and the baby was taken to the resuscitaire. There was silence in the theatre. As the baby girl was premature, the paediatrician had been called to attend in case of emergency and she began checking the baby over. The silence was punctuated by big sobs from Grace. I felt my heart sink. This was not the moment Grace had envisioned. Yes, she was in theatre, which she had wanted, but her legs were in stirrups, and her baby was on the resuscitaire. I knew that this experience would be difficult for her to process. Those minutes must have felt like an eternity. Grace and Dave held hands and tried to comfort one another, but I could see the fear in both of their eyes.

A few puffs of air and the baby girl inflated her lungs, and the silence gave way to an enormous cry. The whole theatre breathed a sigh of relief. The colour came back into Grace's face as she soaked up the sound of her daughter crying. Once the paediatrician was happy with the baby, I wrapped her up and brought her over to meet her parents. Grace felt a little too shaky to be having skin to skin, so Dave leapt at the chance. I placed the baby on her father's chest, covered them in blankets and took some photos of this most precious moment. The little girl blinked her eyes open and looked around. Before long she was licking her lips and rooting around trying to find her way to the nearest nipple. Dave started laughing as his daughter began to wriggle herself round towards his chest. Thankfully Grace had finished having her stitches done, and had been cleaned and transferred to a fresh bed; perfect timing for some skin to skin of her own.

I found myself thinking about Grace for several weeks after this had happened. I'd seen the fear in her eyes when her precious baby had been whipped away onto a resuscitaire and a team of doctors had worked to get her breathing. But more than that, I'd felt the fear in my own body. My emotions felt close to the surface, and it wouldn't take a lot for my heart to start thumping in my chest as my body remembered that maternity does not always have happy endings.

* * *

I fell back into the routine of IVF quickly, still with my original clinic: scans and bloods every other day, injections every evening, sometimes twice a night. The scans were not encouraging, as only one follicle was growing. I tried to remain positive as last time my follicles had taken a while to get going, and then a few more had joined the party.

I felt none of the excitement in my belly that I had the last time. This time I knew that getting pregnant was only the first hurdle. Staying pregnant would be the true test.

Just over a week after the round had started, one follicle had grown enough for egg collection. A nurse called me into a room to discuss the progress and said that I could either cancel the cycle or go ahead with an egg collection with only one follicle. No opportunity was given to speak with a doctor, and I was told I had to make a decision then and there so my egg collection could be arranged if I decided to go that way.

I called James and we decided that we would go ahead with the egg collection. It was worth a shot. That one follicle might give us our baby. Grief and desperation make you do ill-advised things. That night I pinched the fat on my stomach and injected the trigger shot. The one that would in theory make my follicle ready for egg collection in thirty-six hours' time.

This time round, the egg collection was not so much fun. The fancy hospital room and three-course lunch didn't taste as good as before. We had none of the naive hope we had carried with us the first time. No excited nerves, just a dull sadness. This time, when I lay on the anaesthetic table I stared at the ceiling and desperately hoped that this one follicle would produce the goods.

On waking I was told that, yes, there had been one egg in that follicle. Sadly, the next day the embryologist phoned to let us know that it wasn't mature enough and hadn't fertilised. At this point I felt numb. This time I was such a failure that I hadn't even managed to get to the two-week wait. Thousands of pounds, and we didn't even have a chance at a pregnancy. A mere few months ago I had been pregnant with identical twins from one round of IVF, and this time my one egg didn't fertilise.

Hindsight is a wonderful thing. Now, looking back with a lot more experience and knowledge, I know that there was no way that after a week that follicle would produce a mature egg. It was a doomed cycle before it even started. I'm particularly angry that the clinic didn't properly counsel me on the likely outcome. The way the payment worked was that the bulk of the money was for the egg collection. If I didn't go ahead with the egg collection I would be billed for the scans and blood tests, but it would be small fry compared to the thousands of pounds we would pay for the egg collection. I hate to say it, but it felt like they were only after our money.

A week or so later we went back to the clinic for a follow-up. Dr Mali said she was sorry. She recommended checking my AMH again, as my response to the cycle had been a lot poorer than before. At the time I felt like the fight in me had gone out, so I agreed. Again, hindsight is a wonderful thing, but knowing my AMH would not make a jot of difference. AMH only shows the likely response to IVF. At this point we already knew my response had been less than ideal, so putting a number to it was not going to change anything.

When my number came back, as expected it was low. Really low. So low that I knew the odds were stacked highly against us, to the point where I wondered if it would even be worthwhile trying to carry on. During another conversation with Dr Mali, I asked what our plan would be going forwards. She shrugged her shoulders. There was nothing more she could do for us.

Her response immediately ignited a fire within me. I had got pregnant on my first round of IVF, and then I had taken one embryo and made two babies from it. I was not going to sit there and be told that after one failed round there was no hope. I had done something so incredible less than a year ago!

There is one thing that my husband says about me, and that is that I hate not getting what I want. I was so angry that we were being given up on. If Dr Mali didn't want to help us, then I was going to find someone who would.

In the meantime, I was so sad and defeated by the failed cycle that I was signed off sick from work for three weeks to recover. Physically I was fine, but emotionally I was spent. I had pinned all my hopes on being pregnant again as soon as possible. I was finding it difficult to give the energy needed to my patients, while also putting as much as I could into our fight to expand our family. This was all on top of the two-hour commute each way to work since our house move.

On returning to work I sat down with my manager and explained that I wasn't coping. I wanted so badly to be a competent, caring midwife, but I didn't have enough of myself to spread around. During my time off James and I had spoken about many things. In the end, we both agreed that it was in my best interests to return to work, but in a part-time capacity. For me to continue doing the job that I loved, I needed some distance. My manager was so wonderfully accommodating, and it was agreed that I could work three short days each week. It felt like the balance I needed. Enough work for me to get my teeth into (and enough money coming in for us to be able to afford more IVF), but also the space to not let work consume me. On top of that, it allowed me to arrange IVF appointments to fit around my work schedule.

James and I had also discussed the other routes we might take to parenthood. We had not given up on becoming parents, but we knew we might have to think outside the box. We discussed whether we would be open to becoming parents via egg donation. I could still be pregnant, but with the help of a wonderful gift from someone who could produce viable eggs – something I hadn't been able to do in our last round of IVF.

I had experience of looking after couples who were growing their families this way. When I first began my midwifery training egg donation wasn't on my radar. I don't remember seeing it at all. By the time I was on my own IVF journey I was seeing egg donation regularly. Emma was one of the first people I remember seeing who had received donor eggs. She had gone through early menopause in her late twenties. Multiple rounds of IVF with her own eggs had not resulted in a single pregnancy. With her husband, Frank, they had flown to Barcelona to a clinic there where a donor had been found. Frank's sperm had been mixed with the donor's eggs and the resulting embryo had been transferred, leading to Emma's first ever pregnancy.

Emma was of course elated, but it was complicated for her. We chatted about what this meant for her, Frank and their future baby. Emma and Frank had decided they were going to be open with their baby from the beginning about their origins. It was a complicated decision, and Emma told me that she had spent time grieving the fact that her biology wouldn't be passed on. They planned to take the baby back to Barcelona as he or she grew, as they acknowledged it was an important part of their history. They had bought a little onesie with the words 'Made with Love' printed on it, and it brought tears to my eyes. No, Emma was not the genetic mother, but her love would be forever nurturing that child throughout its life.

It was talking to families like this that helped me realise that however James and I arrived at our family, we would be okay. I was still hopeful that we might be able to find another clinic that could help us. I was still furious that our previous clinic had essentially washed their hands of us. It felt like they were kicking us while we were down.

Now that I had reduced my hours at work, I spent every spare minute researching clinics. Most UK clinics will charge for a consultation – around £200 to £300. I narrowed the choice down to three clinics in London that I thought might be a good fit for us. James and I also decided that it might be worth pursuing IVF abroad. I had heard from various online forums that this was much cheaper, and sometimes had higher standards of care. I was open to trying anything, and if we could wangle a trip away then I was definitely up for that. The expense of IVF had meant we couldn't afford holidays on top, so perhaps this way we could have our cake and eat it.

I had seen some patients who had received unethical advice from abroad so knew that we'd need to be cautious. I'd seen some women having to reduce their pregnancies after having several embryos transferred and becoming pregnant with multiple babies. Unlike the UK, which is regulated by the Human Fertilisation and Embryology Authority (HFEA), some countries have little to no regulation of IVF practices and clinics.

I found three clinics in Greece that appeared to be popular and which I thought seemed like they would be suitable. Unlike UK clinics, they all provided free virtual consultations. The first one, in Athens, had an almost cult following in the various IVF forums I was a member of. But while the doctor we spoke to was professional and recommended various tests, one action they suggested included sending off a sample of my period blood in the post to Greece. This seemed like an outdated test to me, and I didn't get a good feeling from the meeting.

The next clinic was in Thessaloniki, and although this one was more positive, it still wasn't quite hitting the mark.

In the meantime, we visited the clinics on my list in London. Having done so much research, I realised that we needed a clinic where our case would be handled by one person only. At our previous clinic I'd seen a different nurse every time I went in, and during the actual cycle you wouldn't see a doctor until the egg collection, and even then it would likely be someone you hadn't met before. It felt like a conveyor belt. I wanted one person to take sole responsibility. I knew from my own experience that if someone was in charge, they were more invested in your case and more likely to make sure that you were receiving the best care.

The last London clinic we saw had been recommended to me by a midwife friend and colleague. I really trusted her opinion as she was an extremely talented and experienced midwife. As soon as I met the doctor I was drawn in. He really knew his research. He took all my concerns seriously and suggested we try something called 'embryo banking'. This is where you undertake several rounds of IVF, but at the end of each one, instead of transferring an embryo, you freeze any embryos you have. This way you can build up a little collection before transferring any back. This appealed to me. Instead of doing one egg collection at a time and transferring whatever was available, I could keep collecting them, which ensured I was as young as possible at the time of collection. This also meant that we would not have to go through the emotional rollercoaster of waiting for potential disappointment and building ourselves back up again each round.

This doctor stated that he was not remotely worried that my AMH was so low. He said the only number that was important was my age. At thirty years old, even if I wasn't producing many eggs, the quality should be reasonable, which would hopefully give us the best chance at achieving a pregnancy. I left feeling positive.

The third Greek clinic we spoke to was also in Thessaloniki, just next door to the other Greek clinic. The doctor we spoke to was fantastic, and I felt very confident that they would be able to help us. One thing that was still playing on my mind was scarring from the retained placenta. My old clinic hadn't wanted to do a hysteroscopy* to see what was happening inside my womb, but I couldn't shake the feeling that something wasn't quite right. This Greek clinic said they

---

* A more accurate version of a HyCoSy, where a camera is inserted into the womb.

would offer the hysteroscopy.

After a discussion, James and I decided we would go and visit the clinic. It seemed sensible to meet them in person before deciding to sign up to any care. This way I could also have the hysteroscopy at a much cheaper price than if we paid to have it in the UK.

And a holiday! We could have some time together just the two of us. We found a boutique hotel that was reasonably priced, booked the cheapest flights we could find and we were off. It seemed like the most bizarre holiday I had ever had. I was flying to a country where I didn't speak the language to be sedated and have a camera inserted into my womb.

I hoped one day I would be able to tell my future child all I had done to bring them into the world.

16

The IVF Holiday

The last time we had been to Greece was the week before we started our first round of IVF, which had led us to Cecil and Wilfred. Now, just over a year later, we were flying there again, but this time to meet with another IVF clinic.

Our flight was late at night, as this was the cheapest option and we were trying to be savvy with money. Undergoing more IVF meant that every penny counted, but we also wanted to try to enjoy being together while we were away. As we were only going for three nights, we decided not to take any hold luggage. I crammed my hand luggage as full as I could with clothes, toiletries and other essentials. It was January, which was irritating because jumpers take up a lot of room!

We sat separately on the flight because we hadn't reserved our seats – again trying to save money where we could. James was quite pleased with this, as he could sit and read his book in peace instead of me trying to bother him with questions.

We were up early the next morning, ready to go to the clinic. But before heading out, we climbed the stairs to the rooftop breakfast room. We indulged in pastries, fruit, cheese, ham and fresh juice. With full bellies, we called a cab to take us to the outskirts of the city for our appointment at the clinic.

The area was somewhat industrial, with other IVF clinics and medical centres nearby. The clinic itself was all white with bright-blue accents. It reminded me of a posh dentist. Everything was gleaming and shiny. The waiting room was busy with Greek clients. Ours was the only English accent I noticed while we were waiting.

The patient coordinator came and greeted us. We were taken to her office where she went through proceedings. She explained how IVF at the clinic worked, what the clinic would offer and that she would be our point of contact while we were in Greece.

A short while later we were taken to meet Dr Nikos, who had conducted our virtual appointment. Just as he had been on screen, he was reassuring and confident that they would be able to assist us. He drew up a plan, which included lots of blood tests. We agreed that I would return the next day for my hysteroscopy.

Our final introduction that day was with Katarina, the nurse. She explained that she was going to take my blood. She laid out around twenty different blood bottles. On seeing my face, she instructed me not to be scared. It wasn't for comfort; it was an order. She was friendly, but I knew she wasn't to be messed with.

Katarina reminded me of Sofia, a client I had caseloaded through her pregnancy. We had met when she was eight weeks pregnant. She had told me immediately she was having a caesarean, before we had even finished our introductions. She was extremely straight-talking and no-nonsense. If she wanted something, she would get right to the point. Throughout the pregnancy she began to soften, and by the end, she had decided she was going to have a water birth in the Birth Centre. Quite the turnaround from her original wish for a surgical birth.

The appointments were always engaging and kept me on my toes. Sofia would always come armed with the latest research, asking how it would relate to her and her baby. I loved talking to someone who was so thorough and interested in learning about the evidence base.

During her labour and birth she was an absolute goddess. She called me to say she had been admitted to the Birth Centre. When I arrived the room was beautiful. The lights had been dimmed and there were electric tea lights dotted round. There were affirmations printed onto posters and stuck to the walls, and a hypnobirthing track was playing in the background.

Sofia was in the pool; her partner, Erik, was massaging her shoulders. During each contraction Sofia would take long sucks on the gas and air, and then after the contraction she would rest her head on the side of the pool, her long, dark hair pulled back off her face.

Sofia was sniffing some lavender essential oil from a flannel, which was giving the room a calming atmosphere. The room was so relaxing that I kept having to remind myself that I was at work. Being privy to something so magical was enough to give me a real high. Experiences like this really affirmed why I was a midwife. It was so I could facilitate other women to be the best they could be. So they could harness the power they had within them to birth their babies in the way they wanted. It was to keep mum and baby as safe as possible during this transition earthside.

As the labour progressed Sofia was becoming more vocal. I could see that Erik was finding it difficult to see Sofia in so much pain. He kept asking if she wanted to try the epidural. In between the contractions Sofia sternly told him that she would let him know if she wasn't coping. Even during labour Sofia was able to speak her mind, and I admired her resolve. A few hours later, a beautiful girl with long, dark hair was born quietly into the water and floated up into her mother's arms.

Later on, after tea and toast and lots of newborn cuddles, Sofia turned to me with a sparkle in her eye. 'I did it!' she exclaimed. I replied that I'd had no doubt she had it in her to birth her baby in such a beautiful and calm way.

Back to Greece, and Katarina had successfully filled twenty vials with my blood. When confirming my details she asked what my father's name was, as is common in Greece to differentiate between patients with the same or similar names. She then explained that I would need an electrocardiogram (ECG)* if I was going to have my hysteroscopy tomorrow. Unfortunately, the clinic didn't perform ECGs, so I would have to go to a local hospital to have it done. The receptionist called a cab for us, and James and I took the ten-minute cab journey to the local hospital. It was on the waterfront, and had a steady stream of people entering and leaving. We walked into the main foyer and already it couldn't have been more different to the IVF clinic. There were people everywhere. The building itself looked run down and had none of the relaxed, calm atmosphere of the IVF clinic.

Katarina had explained that I would be able to find a door in the foyer with a heart sign on it, and I could get my ECG done there. We found the room, and I knocked on the door and waited. A middle-aged woman opened the door and said something to me in Greek. I had no idea what she'd said, so instead I said, 'ECG?' Several Greek sentences were given in response. The woman must have seen my confused face, as she pointed across the foyer to a kiosk. It was the cashier's desk – I needed to pay for my ECG before I could have it done.

The queue was long, but it moved quickly, and once at the front I again asked for an ECG. Unlike at the clinic, English was not spoken by all the staff, and they seemed frustrated by our lack of understanding. Clutching a receipt for the €10 I'd paid, I went back to the original room and knocked.

The lady told James to wait outside and gestured for me to follow her. She gesticulated that I should remove my top and sit down. There was no curtain to change behind, and the lady made no efforts

---

* An electrocardiogram (ECG) is a test to check the heart.

to move or look away. I took my top off and sat on the couch. She wheeled the machine towards me, and I nearly laughed. It looked so old-fashioned, almost like a machine that someone might have made in their garage to try to talk to aliens. Surely this wasn't going to be looking at my heart? It turned out, it was. She connected the wires to me and pressed some buttons while it took its reading.

The whole time, while I was sitting in just my bra, what felt like the entire waiting room kept coming in. No attempts were made to protect my dignity, so I just sat there, hoping it would be over quickly. I was given a piece of paper, which I then had to take to a third place to be signed, and then I was free to go.

James and I laughed as we walked along the waterfront back into town. I'm sure you wouldn't be able to get anything for €10 at a hospital in the UK. Although healthcare is free at the point of delivery on the NHS, the cost of delivering it is incredibly high. Sometimes at work when restocking the store cupboard, I would see the labels on all the products. They would have the barcode, and underneath would be the price. I always found it fascinating, but also shocking, how much everything cost. It certainly used to make me think about the equipment I was using.

We spent the rest of the day sightseeing and enjoying the holiday part of our trip. The food in Thessaloniki was incredible, and knowing I had to fast overnight for my hysteroscopy the next day made me indulge even more.

* * *

An early night, followed by an early start the next day. James went up to breakfast by himself. I was fasting and didn't fancy watching him eat the delicious pastries while nothing could pass my lips. Another cab ride, and we were at the clinic bright and early.

I left James in the waiting room and was taken downstairs into a room that I guessed was a sort of ward. It was a long, thin room with beds lined up along one side. These weren't like hospital beds; they were single beds that you might find in someone's house. They were all neatly made with a thin duvet and pillows all with the clinic branding on. The curtains were all open, and I saw another lady sitting on the side of her bed in her gown, and I also saw two nurses escorting a woman back to her bed and tucking her up. I assumed she had just had a transfer and was feeling a little sore, hence the need for help.

I was instructed to get changed into a gown, and then I walked down the ward into the small theatre. A couch with stirrups was in the middle, and the theatre assistant instructed me to jump up. Katarina was there again, and there were a few other people bustling around. There was nowhere to put my legs other than in the stirrups, so I had to sit there with my vagina exposed for what felt like three hours while everything was prepared.

Someone tried to cannulate me a few times before it was successful, and it all seemed a little chaotic. Eventually the team seemed ready, and although I knew they were all going to see my vagina anyway, I definitely could have done without everyone having a pre-show. Dr Nikos walked in, and I knew that meant it was time to get this show on the road. They had all been talking to each other in Greek while getting everything ready. I appreciated that they were speaking their own language, but it was frightening not being able to understand anything, knowing that I was about to be put to sleep. As I watched the drugs being injected into my vein, I prayed that flying to another country to be sedated while having a camera inserted into my womb wouldn't prove to be a mistake.

* * *

When I woke, I was back in the bed on the ward. These beds

didn't have wheels, so I had absolutely no idea how I had got there. I asked Katarina and she said I walked, as if it was entirely obvious. I blinked. How had I walked there? I had only just woken up. I remembered the nurses helping the patient earlier and decided that must have been how I got there. It was a very unsettling feeling knowing that I'd actually done things while asleep. I hoped I hadn't said or done anything embarrassing.

A short while later, I was asked to get dressed, and then I was taken back upstairs to a lounge. James was waiting for me, and I was relieved to see him again. I wasn't sure what we were waiting for, and at this point I was starving. Dr Nikos appeared and showed us into an office. He produced a USB stick out of his pocket and explained that my hysteroscopy had been filmed. He plugged it into his laptop and then proceeded to show us the video. I'm surprised I didn't burst out laughing at how surreal it all was. I was still high as a kite from all the drugs and James had absolutely no idea what he was looking at, and still we sat there with straight faces while we had a virtual tour of my womb, which thankfully appeared normal.

Once our uterine screening was over, we headed back to the hotel. In our room James started laughing and said he needed to tell me how bizarre it had been while I was in theatre.

We had agreed that he would give a semen sample, so he could undergo something called a DNA fragmentation test. This is a more advanced test than a regular semen analysis and was much cheaper to do in Greece. Katarina had called him down to a room while I was in recovery. She'd explained that he needed to provide a sample. The clinic was thorough, and he had to confirm his details. Name, date of birth and, just before she left him to his business, she asked him to confirm his father's name. Not exactly the mental image you want before you are about to masturbate into a pot. Once he had managed to rid his head of his dad's name and was ready to 'perform', he looked down and saw his dad's name on the pot staring back at him. How he managed to do the sample I'll never know.

By the time James finished telling me, I was rolling around on the bed laughing so much I was worried I might have done some internal damage. I would never wish infertility on anyone, but it was moments like this that made me realise there was no one else I would rather be wading through the mud with.

Our final day was spent sightseeing and trying to inject some normality into our trip. We ate far too much, but also walked and chatted. So far, we were united in our determination for a family. Without James there to lean on – sometimes physically, but mostly emotionally – I'm not sure how I would have got through it all.

As we flew back, I reflected on our trip. The staff at the IVF clinic had spoken perfect English, but our trip to the local hospital had made me realise how fortunate we were to receive healthcare in our native language. I began to think about how frightening it must be for patients who are treated in the UK when English isn't their first language. Having to navigate a medical system that you don't understand in a language that isn't your mother tongue is no easy feat. Working in London meant that seeing patients who didn't speak the language was a routine part of the job. I don't think I had truly recognised how vulnerable those patients were until this experience, when I was in a comparable position.

I thought back to Cho, whom I had looked after on the postnatal ward. She had come to the UK with her husband, who was doing a PhD. Cho didn't speak any English other than 'please' and 'thank you'. From my perspective, it was very difficult trying to communicate with her, as there was much that I wanted to say and ask, but I knew much of it would not be understood. It was always difficult to get face-to-face interpreters to come to the ward, so we relied on a telephone translating service. This was fine for appointment-based services but far more difficult in a ward environment. I will admit that often I would rely on Google Translate on my phone.

It may have made my working day more challenging, but that was nothing compared to how Cho must have been feeling. I can only imagine how isolating it must have been for her, not being able to ask questions or understand what was going on. Being an inpatient in a hospital with a new baby, while also recovering from birth, is tiring for most people. New parents will often have a plethora of questions, but Cho was unable to ask any. I tried to communicate through other ways, by demonstrating what I meant and by smiling. Fortunately, there are lots of resources that have been translated into other languages that I could give to her, but it was no replacement for a proper conversation. We are unable to rely on partners for translating services either, as outside of visiting hours Cho was alone.

I wondered whether Cho had a support network around her, and whether she would find any other mums she could chat to. Having a newborn baby is hard work and can be relentless. Having a network of other mums around you who are going through a similar thing – the cluster feeding, the sleep regressions – can be invaluable.

From my time in Greece, I realised that a friendly face really can put someone at ease despite a language barrier. It costs nothing to smile and really helps to reassure the patient. I hoped I could take this experience and make my practice better. I didn't like how vulnerable it made me, being in a room with everyone speaking a different language. IVF was never something I wanted to be doing, but it was certainly helping me to be a much better midwife along the way.

Once home, James and I took a week or so to mull over the clinics we had visited. There were pros and cons to all of them. They all had something to offer us, so we were nit-picking between them. In the end it became clear which clinic was right for us. Although travelling to Greece had mostly been a positive experience, we decided that we would be better suited to receiving care in London. After meeting with six clinics, there was only one doctor who had asked Cecil's and Wilfred's names. That was the doctor I wanted looking after us.

17

Rotting Eggs

Once we had decided on our new clinic, I was ready to get started with the treatment as soon as possible. Patience had never been my strong point, and every moment without a baby in my arms felt like a moment when I was failing.

We met with our new doctor, Dr Georgiou, to go over the plan. Embryo banking meant that we would undergo three rounds of IVF back to back without a break. At the end of each round any embryos would be frozen and at the end of the fourth cycle I would have an embryo transferred. (I also had the option to have a break at that point if I was feeling too exhausted, and to then undergo a frozen transfer at a later date.)

I began taking my medication. This time I started on oestrogen, which was being used to 'prime' my ovaries and hopefully encourage follicles to grow at a similar rate. I was a week into taking my medication when at work and on the television whisperings began of a virus in China. I vividly remember talking to patients during the day, chatting about what we were hearing on the news. As the week went on things seemed to get more and more serious.

I attended an appointment with Dr Georgiou, who took me into his office and asked whether I had been watching the news. I confirmed that I had, but I was still a little confused. He explained that most hospitals were cancelling all non-emergency treatment, and that because I was still in the early stages of the cycle it would be best to cancel. He said that if I carried on, there was no guarantee that by the time I reached the egg collection there would be an anaesthetist available to perform the sedation.

I felt the desperation rising inside me. I had been wanting to start IVF ever since Cecil and Wilfred had been born. I had last held them almost a year ago and now I was being told that there were going to be further delays. It took all my strength not to throw myself on the floor and have a tantrum at how unfair it was.

By the time I got home I had managed to calm myself down, and I realised that there was a bigger picture here. I stopped taking my medication and resigned myself to the fact that there would be more waiting. At this point I was years into the waiting game, so I convinced myself I could wait a few more months. I had taken two weeks of annual leave, which I was hoping would allow me to fully immerse myself in all things IVF-related. Instead, I began to think of things I could do to cheer myself up.

Within days James was in bed with a fever. Testing hadn't been rolled out yet, and there was no way of knowing whether he had simply come down with ill-timed flu or whether it was coronavirus. With James being unwell, I felt slightly better about the decision to cancel our cycle, as there was no way we could have gone ahead. As always, I struggled with feeling out of control, so any way I could try to rationalise what had happened made me feel calmer.

We spent the next two weeks isolating at home. My parents dropped off a food bundle, and my mum kindly went and bought us some paint. Once James was feeling a little better, we painted the lounge. We had spent so long only thinking about IVF, but now that had been taken away we could think about other things. It all seemed like a big adventure. I wasn't used to having James at home so much, as he usually worked long hours at the pub. Although we were confined to our home, save for solitary dogs walks for me, I enjoyed spending time with him.

Our isolation coincided with my annual leave, and once it was over I returned to work. I was getting more and more questions about Covid-19 each day from patients. Understandably our patients were worried for themselves and their babies. Pregnant women were put on the vulnerable list and advised to shield. Days later the country went into lockdown. James was furloughed from his job running a pub, and I began to drive to work instead of commuting by train. Dressed in PPE, work was intense. Women were attending their appointments alone, often putting their partners on video calls. I ran late for appointments as there was a much longer cleaning regime in between each appointment.

My patients were often scared. Scared that they would have to give birth alone. Scared that they would be left on the postnatal ward alone with a newborn baby that they didn't know how to care for. Scared that they would catch Covid-19 while in hospital and it would be passed on to their baby. It was a worrying time for all of us. Some of my colleagues volunteered to work upstairs in the intensive therapy unit (ITU). As I hadn't trained as a nurse before midwifery I didn't feel confident enough to volunteer, and knew I would be best suited to staying in maternity, keeping mums and babies safe.

I also worried I would catch Covid-19. I didn't develop any symptoms even though James had likely had it. We had slept in the same bed, as we only had one bed in the house, and I had been fine. I felt this had been a lucky escape and it was only a matter of time until I came home with it. I stopped using public transport completely to try to limit my exposure. Thankfully the roads were pretty empty, so what would have been a two-hour drive to work only took an hour. When I got home from work, James would leave the doors open so I could walk straight through and into the bathroom and shower without touching anything. My clothes would go straight into the wash, and once I was clean I would then hug James and tell him all about my day.

I often wanted to cry, especially for the first-time mums. They had never navigated the world of maternity services before, and had to do so alone. Mask-wearing meant I perfected the art of 'smizing' and tried to smile through my eyes as much as possible. I tried to reassure as often as I could. Everyone was working so hard to keep everyone safe, and we knew it wasn't the ideal situation. Not being able to facilitate families to be together during these precious hours and days was not how midwives like to work. Many, many women would attend the hospital for appointments and tell me that they wanted a home birth, as they couldn't bear the thought of giving birth alone. Despite my reassurances that it was very unlikely they would need to birth alone, the media reports that partners were banished did nothing to assuage their nerves.

At the end of the day I would return home tired and sweaty. The masks, not to mention the come-down from starting and then stopping my IVF medication, made my face break out in spots. Selfishly, I would sometimes despair and still think that I would give anything to be having a baby even in the middle of a global pandemic. Even if it meant going to scans and appointments alone, or giving birth alone, or that my newborn baby couldn't meet any of my family, I would have done it in a heartbeat. I knew it would have been anything but easy to be pregnant or a new parent in a pandemic, but I also knew that my heart still ached for a family.

Seeing handmade rainbows in the windows during my dog walks, which were meant to unite us and bring joy, made me feel sad. There was no little person to paint us pictures to hang in the windows. I still felt pangs of sadness when I heard people moaning about having to home-school while working. My house and arms were empty. I knew deep down that there was a responsibility to keep the population safe, and any non-emergency treatment had to be cancelled. I really did understand this, especially as I worked in the NHS. I knew it couldn't be changed, but that didn't make it hurt any less.

The days and weeks wore on. I got used to my new routine. Drive to work, spend all day in PPE, try to keep as much normality as possible for the mums, while also knowing that everything was so very far from normal. Antenatal classes made their way online. In some ways, it was a relief that parents-to-be were still able to access information. It was also desperately sad that they were missing out on the opportunity to make friends. A big part of antenatal classes is meeting other couples who are expecting a baby at a similar time to you. Building your village when you have a baby is invaluable. Knowing other people who are going through something similar at the same time as you can really bond you together. Having someone at the end of a text message in the middle of the night when it feels like the whole world is asleep is priceless.

One day when I came into work there was much chattering among my colleagues. A pregnant patient had been admitted to ITU. I think this was the moment when I fully realised how dangerous Covid-19 was. I didn't know anyone personally who had been badly affected. I had spoken to many patients who were calling up for advice after testing positive, but this was the first time someone had been seriously unwell. On top of that, she didn't have any significant risk factors that would make her a candidate for being so unwell. It was a worrying time. I'm happy to report that she eventually made a full recovery and went home with her baby. During her stay the entire unit was invested in her recovery. There was celebration among all the staff when she left the hospital. The world may have felt like it had been turned upside down, but NHS staff have the most incredible ability to pull together in times of need. That isn't to say that the system within which we work isn't sometimes gruelling, but the spirit of the staff is what holds the entire infrastructure together.

Alongside the rest of the nation, James and I were staying at home and missing out on seeing our friends and family, but we were also still grieving for our boys. Pre-Covid-19, we had decided to throw a party to celebrate Cecil and Wilfred's first birthday. It might seem unusual to hold a party for two little boys who had passed away, but we wanted Cecil and Wilfred to be celebrated, and it seemed like a wonderful way of getting all our closest family together. We had sent out invitations and started buying bits and pieces, like decorations. When Covid-19 hit, we had no choice but to cancel the party and I was hit with another wave of grief. My sons would never have a party because they were dead. Here I was, trying to give them the celebration they deserved, and we weren't even able to go through with that. Many tears were shed out of frustration and sadness.

In the end, James and I spent the day just the two of us. We made an afternoon tea from scratch and sat looking through our photographs of them. We spent a long while looking at all the tiny details of them that had faded from my immediate memory. The tiny shapes of their fingernails, the way they held their arms in exactly the same way as each other, the perfect cupid's bow they both had. We spoke about how sad we were that they didn't get to stay, but how happy we were to have been able to know them, even if it was only for a little while.

Anniversaries of death can be difficult. A whole year had passed, but it felt like just yesterday that I was living through those excruciating moments. At the same time, I felt so sad that I was no closer to giving them a living sibling. The emptiness I felt all the time was heightened. I felt angry that we had wasted a whole year and there was still no baby. I desperately missed Cecil and Wilfred, and no other baby would replace them. However, losing them was the worst period of my life, and only exacerbated my longing for motherhood. I had been so close, only for it to be snatched away.

* * *

Some two months later, the HFEA gave the green light that clinics could begin to operate again. I was euphoric. As soon as I heard the news I was on the phone to my clinic trying to book myself back in. I knew there would be a backlog of other patients whose treatment had been delayed and I didn't want to be forgotten about. I was given the green light to start taking my medication as soon as it was the right time in my cycle, and finally I felt like I was getting my life back on track.

I started taking hormone replacement therapy (HRT – oh, the irony of taking medication aimed at helping the menopause while I was desperate for a baby) and then waited for my period to come. It was an odd moment. I had spent years wishing my period wouldn't come, and here I was hoping it would come as soon as possible.

When it finally arrived, it was time to get this show on the road.

This first cycle, Dr Georgiou explained, we could treat almost as a test run. We would try a new protocol with very mild stimulation, but if this round didn't yield the best results, we still had two further rounds planned and could therefore tweak the medication.

My line managers had been fantastic and said I could take any time off I needed for appointments. As I was part-time by this point I tried as much as I could to have my scans on my days off, but it didn't always work that way.

A week after starting my stimulating medication I went for a scan, only to find that one follicle had shot ahead and was much bigger than the others. This is not ideal, as if you get one lead follicle it can sometimes suppress the growth of any others. A few days later the smaller follicles were not growing very much, but the larger one was nearly ready for collection. As I had so few follicles growing Dr Georgiou decided we could try something a little off-plan.

We would aim for an egg collection to try to retrieve the one large follicle, but then five days after the egg collection I would start stimulating medication again to try to encourage the remaining follicles to grow. This is known as DuoStim or luteal phase stimulation.

I loved that Dr Georgiou was trying to harness every single follicle that I had, and I loved that he was willing to think outside the box to get us the embryos we needed. This extra stimulation meant that I would now be doing four egg collections back to back. I was just so happy to be able to go through IVF again after the delays from Covid-19, and knowing I had four chances for my body to make a golden egg. I had a good feeling. Knowing that Dr Georgiou was really invested in our care was so reassuring. Unlike at my last clinic, nearly every single time I went to my new clinic I saw Dr Georgiou. He performed almost every single scan, or if he couldn't make the scan he would come and see me afterwards with the plan. He did three out of the four of my egg collections and was incredible throughout. He was always so brilliant at managing our expectations, and was also able to think positively and hopefully while being realistic.

The night before the egg collection I was excited. I had grown to love the feeling of being sedated. It was something to look forward to, a lovely relaxing sleep, after a few weeks of injections and hormones.

My last clinic had been very fancy, with the three-course lunch afterwards. I knew my new clinic was not like this at all, so I made sure I packed lots of biscuits!

We were shown through into the pre-op area. The usual checks were done, observations taken, consent obtained, then I met with the anaesthetist and a lovely nurse looked after me. James and I were both in good spirits and we joked and messed around while waiting to go through. Once I was laid on the couch, my legs in stirrups, the anaesthetist came and began to slowly inject the white liquid into my veins as I stared up at the ceiling. I said to myself as I drifted off that one day soon I would be staring at the ceiling in theatre as my baby was born. It gave me a warm feeling as I closed my eyes and slept.

When I woke I was told that one egg had been collected and was going to be fertilised with James' sperm. If someone had said to me a few months before that I would be happy with the results of one solitary egg, I'd have laughed. But here I was, counting my lucky stars. I knew this egg had a lot of work to do, but I was so very hopeful.

The embryologist said they would call me on day five to let me know if the embryo had developed enough to be frozen and in the meantime I had a few days' rest before I started the stimulating medication all over again. I loved being able to have treatment again. For over a year since Cecil and Wilfred died I felt hopeless, whereas now I felt like I was actively doing something positive. I hadn't coped well with feeling stationary. Now I was in treatment again, it felt like I was playing catch-up. Another reason I loved being in treatment was because, although I was moving towards having a baby, there was little to no risk of me falling pregnant. I was deeply afraid of being pregnant again, so collecting the eggs and hopefully freezing any embryos we created meant I was closer to becoming a mum, without having to face the emotional turmoil of living through a pregnancy after loss. Although another pregnancy was all I craved, I was terrified that I might end up having to say goodbye to another baby. I knew it would be (hopefully) nine long months of worrying, which nothing could prepare me for.

Five days after my egg collection the embryologist called to say that one good-quality embryo had made it to the freezer. I smiled knowing that something special had happened where a piece each of James and me had joined together and could potentially turn into another baby. That night I injected myself once more, happy in the knowledge that the freezer had its first little deposit.

I felt like I had a spring in my step, and I walked around work with a smile on my face. I knew that going through the IVF process was actually going to be the easy part of our parenthood journey going forward, but I pushed that to the back of my mind and tried to focus on my growing follicles.

One day at work, while I was writing our allocations for the day on the board, a midwife I hadn't seen for a little while came over and asked if I was pregnant. In a room full of people. I felt the smile fall from my face immediately. Of course I wasn't pregnant. I couldn't get pregnant, that was the whole problem. My belly was swollen from hormones, medication and my recent egg collection. This wasn't a sweet little first-trimester bump growing; this was thousands of pounds' worth of drugs that had swollen my ovaries. It took all my might not to scream.

I took some deep breaths and walked off. Thankfully the rest of the day was so busy that it took my mind off her comments. Later that afternoon I saw Anna. Anna was expecting her third and fourth children: twins. I often found it emotionally challenging to look after other people with twins. Not Anna, though. She was so gentle and gracious that it was a pleasure. As Anna had already had two babies before, she wanted to try to give birth to her babies vaginally. This was exciting for me as many twin parents choose to give birth via caesarean, so this was a little different. There's no judgement on parents who choose caesareans from me – that was how I had intended to give birth to Cecil and Wilfred if things had gone to plan – I just found it interesting as something slightly unusual. I knew there was something special about Anna and her babies, and she went on to prove me right by having her twins on different days! I had never seen that happen before. It was having these unusual experiences that kept me coming back to my job, despite the obvious hardships.

* * *

The next egg collection saw three eggs collected. Of these, all three fertilised, and one made it to the freezer five days after egg collection. To my delight, one further embryo was frozen the next day, taking the total up to three. I still had one embryo frozen from the very first round that created Cecil and Wilfred, so the grand total was four embryos.

The third of my four back-to-back IVF cycles was not quite so successful. Yet again, one follicle was growing and one egg was collected. This time the embryo wasn't ready to freeze until day seven, which suggested the quality wasn't going to be great.

At my final egg collection three eggs were collected. One didn't fertilise at all, one fertilised abnormally, but one little one made it all the way to day five. Instead of freezing this one, I had it transferred back into what I hoped was my cosy womb lining.

Two weeks later, at four-thirty in the morning, the blank space where the second line on a pregnancy test should be stared back at me. I was not pregnant. Five embryos remained, but several months of hormones and hopes with not a lot to show for it had worn me down.

We had run out of money, but I knew I had to do another transfer before the year was over. I couldn't go through another Christmas without knowing I'd tried everything to grow our family.

My mum agreed to give us the money for another transfer and I started the process all over again. My first frozen embryo transfer. It was a lot less intense than the egg collections I was used to, though sadly there was no sedation for this.

Once my lining had been thickened by the medication, I was booked in for the transfer. It was December by now. I had started my medication in May and here I was over six months later still filling myself up with hormones.

Covid-19 restrictions were back again, and James couldn't come up for the procedure with me. Instead, he stayed in the coffee shop downstairs while I tried not to think about my overfull bladder. I knew the team very well by this point, after coming into the clinic nearly every other day for months. As they all got ready around me, one of the team asked if I wanted any music on. I decided I wanted to listen to Christmas music. Someone turned a playlist on, and Christmas pop music started to twinkle out.

As Dr Georgiou got the catheter that contained mine and James' embryo ready, I felt a sense of calm. The catheter was fed through my cervix and into my womb. I watched on screen as the embryo was placed into the perfect spot in my uterus. In that moment I felt a real sense of peace wash over me. I knew I had done everything in my power to give us a family.

I left clutching a photograph of our embryo to show James and we drove home and put our Christmas decorations up. It was one of the happiest days we had experienced in months. Now began the two-week wait.

I tried to busy myself with Christmas preparations, but the stakes felt high. I knew I would be a mess if this transfer failed and another year was passing us by. A week later I bled. I was taking such a high amount of progesterone this time, not just the lovely bum bullets, but injections, too, so I knew the bleeding couldn't be due to low progesterone. Perhaps I was pregnant and this was implantation bleeding. I didn't dare let myself acknowledge the thought. I couldn't get carried away, so I emailed Dr Georgiou and asked if we could check my progesterone levels, just in case.

I went to the clinic the next day for a quick blood test, then spent the rest of the day anxiously checking my phone. When it did eventually ring, I was so shocked I nearly dropped my phone. I was sat on the sofa watching television with Crumpet snuggled up on my lap.

Dr Georgiou was on the phone. My progesterone wasn't low, thankfully. I knew what this meant before he even said it.

I was pregnant.

18

Pregnancy After Loss

The first days after my positive pregnancy test dragged by. I felt nervous. I had done the easy part of getting pregnant (said with full irony, as nothing about getting pregnant had been easy) and now I had to do the hard part of staying pregnant for as long as possible. The days of December passed and I tried to busy myself with Christmas. Strict Covid-19 rules meant that we wouldn't be able to mix with our wider family on Christmas Day. We were disappointed, but morning sickness had already started to kick in, and I would be quite happy on the sofa. As I went to bed on Christmas Eve, I pleaded with my body not to miscarry on Christmas Day.

During the day I noticed some light-pink stains in my underwear, and as the day went on the spotting became heavier until it couldn't be ignored. And yet I tried to ignore it, as I didn't want Christmas Day to be marred by the memories of yet another failure. We drove to A&E on Boxing Day morning, and Covid-19 meant that James had to stay in the freezing-cold car, while I sat in the waiting room on my own. I was about six weeks pregnant at this point. I left a few hours later, with absolutely no idea whether I was having a miscarriage or not. We drove home and braced ourselves for the coming hours and days. Either the bleeding would get heavier, or it would stop.

Thankfully it tailed off, and within a few more days we had our scheduled scan at the clinic. Again, James couldn't come with me, so I went alone. Seeing Cecil's and Wilfred's heartbeats together had been such a magical moment, so I was sad for James. I wished he could be there for this scan, assuming we were lucky enough to see a heartbeat this time. In addition, if there was bad news, I would rather he was there to hold my hand through it.

Part of me was hopeful that there might be two heartbeats. I knew the chances of getting pregnant with identical twins twice was very unlikely, but then again, a lot of very unlikely things had happened to me. It was a mix of hope and fear. I felt like I'd been robbed of the chance to be a twin mother. I had imagined the double buggy, the matching outfits, the having to explain who was who. Once that seed had been sown, I wanted it. At the same time, I was terrified of having twins again. Two babies meant more risk. What if my cervix couldn't cope, even after my operation to close it? It was a double-edged sword.

I undressed from the waist down, yet again, and lay back on the couch. One tiny blob with a flickering heartbeat appeared on the screen and I allowed myself to breathe a small sigh of relief. One baby. This was a positive step, but the road ahead of me felt so very long. I took the scan photo downstairs to show James and we drove home happy.

The morning sickness began to ramp up. James was furloughed again due to Covid-19, and this was a blessing. Every moment that I wasn't at work I spent horizontal on the sofa. I had thought that perhaps this time, being pregnant with one baby, the morning sickness might be less than during my twin pregnancy. I was mistaken. The only difference was that I knew what to expect this time, whereas last time it had been such a shock.

Now that the first two waves of Covid-19 were over, having to get the train and tube to work while wearing a mask did nothing to help my sickness. On more than one occasion I arrived at work crying at how unwell I felt. I would plead with my body not to vomit while I was with a patient. I was thankful I didn't have hyperemesis gravidarum (HG), a severe vomiting condition of pregnancy. When I came across patients who were suffering with this it helped put my own condition into perspective.

Louise was pregnant with her second baby. With her first baby she had also experienced HG, and it had left her feeling so traumatised that she had waited six years before having another baby. She had been so debilitatingly unwell that she wasn't sure she could put herself and her family through it again.

Now pregnant again, Louise had originally been seen in the early pregnancy unit, but as her pregnancy had progressed, she was seen within the maternity unit and also in ambulatory care as she would sometimes attend as an outpatient for medication to be administered. Her sickness was so severe that she weighed less during pregnancy than before it. She couldn't work, couldn't look after her six-year-old, could barely manage to get out of bed some days. Not only was she vomiting, but she also had a condition called ptyalism, where she had excessive saliva and would need to spit constantly.

Pregnancy for Louise was a marathon. Simply a means to an end where she could hold her baby in her arms. She vomited every single day of her pregnancy, up until the day she gave birth. She elected to be induced early so the pregnancy would end, along with her suffering. The relief on her face when she finally held her little baby! Not only was she delighted to meet her child, but she had told me that this was to be her final pregnancy. Never again would she be beholden to the challenging condition which is HG.

Even on my most difficult days I tried to remind myself of Louise. I knew my sickness would pass. Despite feeling like I was being punished for something, I tried to make myself feel grateful for every symptom. If Louise could get through her whole pregnancy,

I could do the same. It was an odd feeling, hating being pregnant, while desperately wanting it so badly.

At around ten weeks pregnant I woke early one day and went into the bathroom to find my underwear soaked through with blood. Not spotting this time; it was bright-red, heavy blood. I stumbled back into the bedroom and told James I was bleeding. We drove to A&E, and I was sitting in the waiting room by myself by 6.10 a.m. After several hours of waiting, eventually I was taken round to the early pregnancy unit and scanned – my little blob had grown and was still hanging on in there. Relief flooded through my body. A small area of bleeding had been identified, but nothing more sinister. I walked out of the EPU clutching a scan photo, but I knew it could all change.

The bleeding settled after a week or so, but each day I felt like I was waiting for the worst to happen. Every night when I got into bed I would thank my body and my baby for getting through another day. Each morning when I woke I wondered if this would be the day that it all came crashing down around me.

As the days crept by my fears didn't ease. At thirteen weeks I was due to have a second stitch put into my cervix. This stitch went at the bottom of my cervix and would be removed before my caesarean. With any vaginal suture there is a risk of miscarriage, and I was torn whether to have this second stitch. The permanent stitch I already had should have been enough, but my doctor had recommended it, and I was worried that I might regret not having it done if I then went on to experience premature labour again. I also worried that if I went on to miscarry, I would have caused it myself by having it done. It was a catch-22 of hoping I was doing the best but fearing I was doing the worst.

I had to fast from the night before the procedure, which was not appreciated, as due to my sickness I was waking in the night to snack. I vomited in the car several times on the way to the hospital, mainly because I was so hungry. Still, I tried to tell myself it was all for the best.

I had this procedure on the labour ward at my work. I hadn't told anyone I was pregnant and was doing my best to see as few people as possible to stop the news spreading. The theatre team were great. My spinal numbed me from the waist down. This time, when I lay back in the theatre and stared at the ceiling, I made myself a promise that the next time I was in this very same theatre, I would be meeting my living baby. It was the only thought that kept me going. The procedure itself was over and done with very quickly and before I knew it I was being wheeled out.

I bled for two weeks after the suture. I was scared to move, and barely walked at all. While not heavy, the bleeding was enough to terrify me. Every time I went to the toilet I would dread what I might see. At work, I would try to move as little as possible, as I worried this would bring on extra bleeding. I would be constantly dashing off to the toilets so I could pull down my underwear and inspect what was on my pad. I was so nervous that I was going to miscarry, and it would be my fault for having the second stitch.

I wasn't sure I had the strength to say goodbye to another baby.

The weeks continued to drag past. I started to feel better from the nausea and vomiting. My bump grew and I spoke to the little person living inside me as often as I could. I told her or him that I loved them. That I wanted so desperately to meet them, but not for a few months.

My twenty-week scan came, and we chose not to find out the sex of our baby. We hadn't known the sex of the twins and James had enjoyed not knowing during my previous pregnancy. I had, too, but I also didn't want to find out because I was afraid. I was afraid that knowing the sex of this baby would make them more real. It was frightening to allow myself to fall in love when I was petrified I might have to say goodbye again.

I also had a fear of having another boy. My gut was telling me this baby was a boy, simply because I knew it would upset me. I worried I would look at another baby boy and constantly be comparing him to Cecil and Wilfred. I worried I would see their faces in my new baby. That I would be haunted by them. So it was easier not to know.

The scan was straightforward with no complications, and I momentarily breathed a sigh of relief. I was getting close to the gestation at which I went into labour with Cecil and Wilfred. These next few weeks would be key.

Every day I felt like I was holding my breath. Twenty plus two. Twenty plus four. Twenty plus six. Twenty-one plus zero. Twenty-one plus one. The gestation I gave birth. The day itself was an anticlimax. I felt mostly fine. I knew I was nowhere near safe, but it was a relief to know I had made it further in this pregnancy.

The next few days were uneventful, until I reached twenty-two weeks and promptly lost all composure. I started to feel pelvic pain, similar to the pain I felt in my last pregnancy. I couldn't figure out whether this meant I was going into labour and I would shortly be saying goodbye to another baby. Thankfully, my dad came and drove me to the hospital where I worked. I told him to drop me off outside, and not to wait.

As it turned out, I wasn't going home. I was admitted to the antenatal ward. It took all of my strength not to break down. I think this was partly because I was surrounded by other people, many of whom were my colleagues. It felt like a big deal to let my peers see me at my most vulnerable.

I lay in the ward listening to the noises of the other patients. Two other women in the bay that night were also in for threatened preterm labour. One lady in the bed space next to me was nineteen weeks with twins and her waters had gone. She hadn't gone into labour, but the risk of developing an infection was high. She was from Lithuania and spoke loudly to her friends on the phone while I lay there imagining the worst for us both.

James popped in on his way to work in the morning. He bought clothes, my laptop and other essentials. I tried to remain upbeat, but I was terrified. The rest of the day passed in a blur of ward rounds and observations rounds, dinner rounds, drugs rounds. Barely a moment's peace. My heart felt like it was racing as I sat and analysed every twinge in my body. The pain had remained and I was exhausted from it.

By the evening it all got too much. I picked up my phone, and as I did I snapped my phone charger in two. Nothing major, but in that moment I thought I had lost the ability to call James in an emergency. I knew it would take him an hour in no traffic to get to me if something happened overnight. I sobbed loud, heavy sobs over my broken phone charger. I was lonely and scared, and my phone was my only way to contact James as he tried to work alongside visiting me in the hospital. I was tired and in pain, and fear had taken over my body.

My cries must have been so loud that a colleague popped her head round the curtain and scooped me up in a hug. I was inconsolable by this point. I managed to blurt out a few words:

'My baby is going to die.'

I couldn't help it. The past few months had all caught up with me. I hadn't been fully prepared for how terrifying it would be to be pregnant again after losing Cecil and Wilfred. My kind colleague sat with me until I had calmed down. Then, when I was slightly more composed, she excused herself and came back armed with the consultant, the registrar, the house officer and the midwife in charge.

The consultant tried to reassure me without giving me too much hope. I knew he did not know whether my body was going into labour. I appreciated his honesty and knew that it was out of everyone's control. I was in hospital, taking more progesterone than I ever knew possible to try to prevent me going into labour. My cervix had been sewn up twice. I had done everything in my power, but I still didn't believe that this pregnancy was going to end with a living, breathing baby in my arms.

Overhearing what was going on with all the other patients was only adding to my anxiety. The midwives took pity on me and moved me to a side room. They made sure it was not the same room I was in during my stay with Cecil and Wilfred, which I appreciated. I spent the next few days watching Netflix, napping and wondering whether I was making myself more nervous while being in hospital.

A few days later I was discharged, with no explanation of what the pain was. I just wanted to get to twenty-three weeks, but even though that was a mere few days away, it felt like an eternity. Although (as I've mentioned) 'viability' is at twenty-four weeks, I knew that if I went into labour at twenty-three weeks, the hospital where I worked would be likely to offer resuscitation. I was so close.

Instead of going home, I went to stay with my parents for a couple of weeks. James was working long hours at the pub and I was terrified of being by myself. I kept imagining that my waters had broken, but there was nothing there. I wanted the reassurance of having people around me and especially of knowing that someone would be available to take me back to hospital if needed. I felt like I was so close to viability, but that it could all be taken away from me.

When I did eventually make it to twenty-four weeks, I did not feel the relief I'd wished for. Instead, I still felt petrified. Even if I went into labour at this gestation, yes, the baby would be offered resuscitation, but the chances of survival were poor. I realised that the fear was most likely going to stay with me for the entirety of the pregnancy.

At this point, due to Covid-19, I could no longer be patient-facing at work. Instead, I was tasked with being the e-midwife, who would respond to the many patient emails we received every day. These would range from the amusing to the concerning. The spectrum of questions, enquiries and queries was vast.

From women putting garlic in their vaginas to women wanting advice on nursery equipment and women who wanted to talk through their options for birthing, this new role kept me on my toes.

Questions regarding Covid-19 were plentiful. Whether it was wanting advice on the vaccine, on whether the patient should be shielding, on whether they should avoid family gatherings, on whether their partners were advised to go to work – it went on and on.

Some patients emailed with such concerning symptoms that my heart would beat hard in my chest, and I'd wonder why their first response was to send an email rather than seek urgent medical advice. Often there would be emails with women reporting heavy bleeding in early pregnancy that would sometimes result in miscarriage. The pathways in early pregnancy can be challenging, with women feeling like it is hard to access care. I found that women were so confused about who should be handling their pregnancy losses that they were relying on a non-urgent email service because they felt they had nowhere else to turn. It was upsetting to think that these women didn't have someone they could speak to either face to face or over the phone during what could be an emotional time.

There were other moments of lightness. One patient, Alana, would email every single day with a different question. I quite enjoyed having the time to answer and find the appropriate resources and information to share. Some days it would be asking if she could eat a certain food, other days it might be if she could take an over-the-counter medication. I never met Alana in person, but over a three-month period of being the e-midwife I felt like I got to know her. It felt like she needed a friend, and I was happy to be that person for her.

James started to try to get us prepared for the arrival of our baby. We would need to buy things, even though it felt to me as though buying physical things for our baby would jinx the pregnancy. I didn't want to leave the hospital empty-handed again and then have to come home to a house that was all set up for a baby.

Pram shopping felt so surreal. The sales assistant seemed to have the utmost faith that I would be bringing this baby home. I smiled along as if I felt the same way. I pushed the prams round the shop, not truly believing that I would ever be pushing my own little person round in one. I went through the motions because that was what I was supposed to do. Every time I felt a little flicker of excitement, I would remind myself not to get carried away.

Boxes began to arrive, and I didn't want to open them, so instead I let them build up in piles round the house. At the same time, I decided to distract myself by renovating the house. And when I say 'I', I mean James. I set James to work making sure our house would be ready. I knew the tiny baby wouldn't care at all about the state of the house, but I needed something to focus on that wasn't our baby.

We painted, we got new carpets, we cleaned the roof, we had tiles fixed, we even sanded and stained the wooden floors downstairs.*

We waited until around twenty-five weeks of pregnancy to tell friends and wider family. Our parents and siblings knew, and a handful of friends, but mostly I hadn't been able to face telling people before this point. In fact, I would have quite happily kept the pregnancy a secret until the baby was born, but James wanted to share the news. It wasn't that I didn't want people to know, it was that I didn't really want to talk about being pregnant. It was too difficult for me to process my own feelings, let alone share them with other people.

* * *

At thirty-two weeks, after having a huge number of scans, I went

---

* I did absolutely none of this! I was project manager while poor James was put to work by his emotional and heavily pregnant wife.

for a growth scan alone. We had been to so many scans at this point, and James couldn't get the time off work. At the end of the scan I was told that my baby had a condition called hydronephrosis. This is a kidney condition where one or both of the kidneys is swollen due to an obstruction in the urine flow.

I had seen this condition many times through work, and knew it wasn't anything to be overly concerned about. I wasn't worried about the kidney itself, but instead I was taken back to my pregnancy with Cecil and Wilfred. The last time I had gone to a scan alone, I'd been told that Cecil had talipes. A week later I was in labour and both the babies died. Here I was again, at a scan by myself, being told there was something wrong with my baby. My brain was telling me that within a week this baby was going to die, too. There were too many similarities for me to rationalise that the diagnosis of this problem had very little to do with me going into labour.

The final few weeks of the pregnancy were a slog. The closer I got to my caesarean date, the more worried I became that everything was going to start going wrong. I allowed myself to buy bits and pieces I would need for the birth and postnatal period. I told myself that I would be giving birth, and therefore would need maternity pads and other such items whether this baby lived or not.

Looking back, I can see how very unwell I was at the time. My thoughts were sad and obsessive, and yet I was rejected from the perinatal services three times, with little reasoning given. Perinatal services are a team of experts who specialise in women with mental health conditions who are pregnant or have recently given birth. My midwife referred me several times, and each time I was rejected for not meeting the criteria. There was no support at all unless I wanted to pay for private therapy, which we couldn't afford. I had fantastic midwifery and obstetric input, but these people, my colleagues and carers, were not trained counsellors or therapists.

There were moments of joy and beauty in between all the

worrying. I knew my caesarean was going to be performed early, and I wanted to give myself the best chance of breastfeeding, so I started hand-expressing during the third trimester. With advice and support from a friend and colleague, I started collecting droplets of colostrum, the first breast milk, in little syringes and putting it in the freezer. Twice a day I would sit on the sofa and scoop up these droplets of liquid gold. I was amazed that my body was making milk. It took the pressure off being able to breastfeed straight away, as if for any reason I couldn't feed, I would still have breastmilk to give to my baby. By the time I got round to giving birth I had over 50ml of breastmilk in the freezer – a quite exciting feat, which bolstered my confidence.

I would sit there in the evenings while James was at work and embrace every wriggle, knowing that our baby was growing inside me. Sometimes for a few short minutes I could forget everything that had gone before, and instead marvel at the incredible thing my body was doing.

I tried to do all the things a 'normal' parent-to-be would. I meal-prepped and stocked the freezer. I washed, dried and folded all the tiny baby clothes. I read a couple of parenting books. I sat with James while he did some online antenatal teaching sessions. It didn't feel real.

I chose not to have a baby shower. I had found attending them very difficult over the past few years and didn't want to cause anyone else to feel that way. I also didn't want to have one because it felt too good to be true. A lasting fear during the pregnancy was that I would jinx things, and a baby shower felt like another one of those things. I knew there would be plenty of time to celebrate if we brought this baby home.

My last day of work before maternity leave felt surreal. I left it right to the last possible day, finishing on the Friday, when my caesarean was booked for the Monday. As I was still working from home at this point as the e-midwife, as Covid-19 restrictions meant I could not be patient-facing in the third trimester, there was no final send-off. I went in to work for one last time to have my pre-op assessment and return my work laptop. In just a few days' time I knew I would be back again in theatre. Several years in the waiting, I was finally so close to the end.

The night before, the house was prepped and the bag was packed. We had booked our parking and dropped Crumpet off at my parents' house. I was sure I wouldn't sleep a wink with nerves, but miraculously I fell straight to sleep and awoke on Monday morning to our very early 4.45 a.m. alarm.

I was first on the list that day, so there was very little waiting around. Finding out the baby was now breech, when just a week before he or she had been head-down, brought some lightness to the day.

When James and I finally walked down to the theatre, I still couldn't quite believe we had made it this far. The theatre team were all so friendly and the atmosphere was wonderful. Once numb, I was laid down on the operating table.

I stared at the ceiling as I had done so many times before. It had all led up to this moment. Four years, seven rounds of IVF, tens of thousands of pounds, several operations and the devastating loss of our identical twins.

I held James' hand with nervous excitement and listened. And then I heard the most beautiful noise I've ever heard.

My son's cry.

19

Life After Loss

My third son Percy looked just like his two older brothers. I had feared during my pregnancy that I would be reminded of Cecil and Wilfred every time I looked at my new baby. Instead, I loved looking for the likenesses. It was perfect. Beautiful, sad, complicated, but perfect.

Having a baby did not erase the pain of everything that had come before. I was gloriously happy (and tired), but I also had moments of sadness, when I missed my two eldest boys.

One thing that was unexpected to me was the tidal wave of grief that I felt. The post-birth hormones were wild, and when coupled with the sleep deprivation and the reality of loss, it was an emotional combination. Bringing home a living baby really highlighted everything I had lost when Cecil and Wilfred died. I had to grieve for everything I would miss out on with them. I would never give them their first bath, never get to rock them to sleep or feel their warmth as they slept on my chest. This new grief was one of the strongest I had felt so far. Every new experience we had with Percy I had to mourn never being able to have with his older brothers.

The birth itself was challenging and left me bruised both physically and emotionally. I had expected to walk into an elective caesarean and be wheeled out an hour later, glowing and snuggling my baby. Three hours after walking into theatre I was finally taken to recovery, thankful that this part was over. Trying to ignore the bag which was collecting the blood draining out of my abdomen due to excessive blood loss, we called our families to tell them the good news. They were of course delighted to hear we'd had another son, and so we focused our energy on making sure this new addition to our family was taken care of.

Unexpectedly, breastfeeding came easily to me. Possibly the only part of making or having a baby that did. I was so proud of myself for being able to achieve something that I had desperately wanted to do. I thought I knew a fair amount about breastfeeding after teaching parents and helping mothers for many years. It turned out that I was only scratching the surface.

I had told parents countless times that a baby should feed eight to twelve times in twenty-four hours. This makes me laugh now; I couldn't differentiate the feeds as it felt like Percy would feed eight to twelve times an hour. He was permanently attached to my breasts. He was gaining weight, and I had no pain while breastfeeding, so I felt like it was going well, but it was so very intense. I second-guessed myself constantly. At every weigh-in I anticipated being told that my breastfeeding wasn't good enough and that I would have to stop and formula-feed him. I had nothing against formula feeding, but I wanted to prove to myself that my body could do something 'right' after years of feeling like it had let me down. Infertility had left my self-esteem in tatters and it was hard to believe that something was going well. (The joke is on me, because it turned out that, well over a year later, stopping breastfeeding would in fact be the hard part!)

Life with a newborn was very different to how I'd imagined. Probably because I had never really let myself imagine what it would be like. It was relentless and repetitive. It was unglamorous – the night sweats were next level. I was constantly covered in bodily fluids. Percy would pee and poop every time I took his nappy off. He would posset (a small regurgitation of milk) all down my clothes. I was bleeding, and also my breasts would be pouring with milk, soaking through my top. It was messy, but it was also divine. The smell of him. The tiny squeaking noises he made. When he curled his little fingers round one of mine, he gave me a reason to smile again.

Recovery from the caesarean was easier than I'd anticipated. I was sore, but the pain was manageable, and I was up and walking around again quickly. The lack of strength in my stomach took a while to get used to, and I developed 'mother's thumb' – pain in your thumbs and wrists from picking up and holding the baby – which I'd never heard of and was very painful. I couldn't believe no patients had ever mentioned this to me before – it was so sore! The tiredness was also a shock. I'd previously been frustrated when it seemed that parents had the monopoly on tiredness. Before bringing Percy home, if I'd ever mentioned I was tired, I was met with 'Just you wait ...' while people regaled me with tales of how exhausting life with children is. They weren't wrong; having a newborn was indeed exhausting, but so was living with the uncertainty of whether I would ever bring home a living child.

The hangover from infertility did not immediately resolve once Percy was here. I had intrusive thoughts for quite a long time afterwards. The common theme was that someone was going to take Percy away, or that something bad was going to happen to him. For quite a long time I didn't recognise him. Although I could see a likeness to Cecil and Wilfred, my brain also started to tell me that there had been a mix-up at the IVF clinic, and that the wrong embryo had been put back. I couldn't see either myself or James in Percy and was worried that someone was going to come and claim our baby as theirs. I did vocalise to family members that this was happening, but not to any healthcare professionals. I'm not sure why; perhaps I had lost faith that any mental health support would be provided as I had not received any during the pregnancy. Thankfully these thoughts lessened over time, but it was challenging to live with, and I was glad when James started working from home so that I didn't have to be by myself.

The realities of motherhood were eye opening, and I knew my midwifery practice would be changed for the better. All my children had changed me as a midwife. Each time I learnt new things about myself, it helped me to consider the bigger picture and how I could help other women.

I remembered Jo, a mother I cared for at home, saying to me that her baby never wanted to be put down. I told her about the fourth trimester (the first twelve weeks with your newborn baby) and how babies wanted to be close to their mothers as this was a survival instinct. The baby had spent nine months inside their mother, and so being apart from them was scary for them. When Jo and many other mothers told me the baby wouldn't be put down, I don't think I truly understood what they meant. I thought that you fed the baby, wrapped them up and then put them in the Moses basket until they woke a few hours later for another feed. I had seen countless babies asleep in their cribs and assumed this was how all babies behaved. I remember performing a check-up on Jo's baby, then swaddling the baby and laying them down to sleep. Jo seemed surprised that the baby had settled and told me this didn't happen with her. I showed her my swaddling technique and assumed this would help.

Percy did not want to be put down either (and still doesn't). At all. I thought back to Jo and the desperate looks she had given me. I hadn't appreciated that when she had told me her baby didn't want to be put down, she had really meant it. Percy could be fast asleep, but the second I put him in his Moses basket he would cry and cry. I didn't understand it. I had fed and changed him, and I had cuddled him; surely he didn't want to be touching me the entire time. Those first few weeks (and then months) I survived on a couple of hours of broken sleep per night. I think in total Percy spent about one hour of his whole life in that Moses basket. It sat practically untouched in our lounge as no matter what I tried, I could not put him down. It was humbling to realise that I had probably come across as entirely unhelpful during my home visit to Jo and many others.

The stream of visitors to our house in the first few weeks after Percy's arrival was exhausting, but also wonderful. Seeing our family fall in love with this tiny baby was magical. In particular, seeing our parents with their grandchild was very special. I had felt like I'd been letting my parents down over the years with my inability to produce a grandchild, and getting to see them love and cherish Percy as much as I do is one of the best parts of welcoming him into our family. I took such pleasure in getting him dressed every day, then sending them an OOTD (outfit-of-the-day) picture. One of my favourite memories is of dressing Percy in a babygrow that I wore as a baby.

Apart from the obvious part of loving having a baby, I loved not being pregnant anymore. The responsibility for keeping Percy alive was no longer mine alone; I could share the load. James was an excellent father, as I knew he would be. He was also a brilliant partner throughout our whole journey to parenthood. Watching him fall in love with our boy was beautiful. Seeing him singing to Percy or just snuggling with him made me both swell with love, but also feel such sadness that we'd missed out on these moments with Cecil and Wilfred.

As I hadn't gone to antenatal classes, I didn't have the ready-made set of friends that those classes can often bring. Instead, I met a few mums through a parenting app, and then my friendships grew from there. One thing I found hard to navigate was the 'Is he your first?' question that I faced every time I met someone new. Invariably I said yes, as I didn't want to dampen the conversation with someone I was hoping would be my friend. Percy was the first baby that I was mothering in the physical sense.

I think all parents go through a period of adjustment as they try to navigate this new world they find themselves in – it's a huge change, after all – and we were no different, just with a little extra baggage. I was working out whether I was a first- or third-time mum, or both. Deciding who I could trust with my story. Wondering whether my nerves were normal first-time-mum nerves or whether they were due to four years of heartache.

There were, and still are, hard parts of parenting, but I try to cherish as much of it as I can. I, of course, find myself getting frustrated, or worried, but mostly I am filled with a sense of gratitude. I can't forget the feelings I had when I was unsure if I would ever be a mother to a living baby. The smallest moments mean the most to me. Simple things like pushing the pram, hearing Percy call me 'Mummy', or when he snuggles in for a cuddle. My heart simultaneously swells with love, but also aches with sadness for my older two boys.

I now know that grief is a life sentence. I will never stop grieving for Cecil and Wilfred because I will never stop loving them. This no longer makes me sad; instead, I am grateful for the lasting impact they have had upon my life. The fact that they lived, even for such a short time, has brought me more joy than I thought possible.

I am a mother to three boys. One who I hold in my arms, and two who I carry in my heart.

Afterword

When I read back over the events of the past few years of my life, I am sometimes amazed that I made it through it all. The catalogue of disasters I encountered would seem almost laughable if they weren't so heartbreaking, too. The saddest part for me is knowing that other people also experience this devastation.

Having a baby is not a cure for infertility. I am still infertile and the effects of it are longer lasting than I anticipated. I naively thought that once I was holding a living baby all the trauma from the past few years would be forgotten and healed. Instead, it was amplified. I know now there will always be a dull ache in my heart from the longing to hold two little boys tightly.

I made a choice to embrace all the positive things that Cecil and Wilfred have brought to my life, rather than mulling over all I have lost. Their gift to me, and their legacy, shines through in everything I do, but it would be remiss to pretend that their absence from my life doesn't continue to devastate me.

As detailed throughout this book, my mental health took a battering over a long period of time. I have found that there are so few services available to those who experience loss and infertility, and as with IVF, there is a postcode lottery to boot. I was ploughing so much money into having a baby that I simply couldn't afford to spend any more on private counselling. I was fortunate enough to receive a few counselling sessions from a local charity, and although it was of some help, it was nowhere near the level of support I really needed.

As a result I was never diagnosed with any mental health conditions, and when I fell pregnant with Percy I found again that there was a huge lack of support, as my referrals from my midwife to my local perinatal team were rejected on more than one occasion. I know services are underfunded and underresourced, but I was crying out for help. I had a fantastic midwife and obstetrician looking after me, but there was no one there to help me process the huge emotions I was feeling.

On a basic level, I would love for midwives to be taught about IVF during their training. Given that so many couples walk into the maternity department having undergone fertility treatment, it still shocks me that midwives learn so very little about this.

Although most midwives and doctors are compassionate, the lack of education on this subject sometimes means there is a gap in understanding and a lack of empathy when it comes to loss and infertility. To the practitioner it is every-day and routine, but to the patient undergoing IVF and the subsequent pregnancy it is a once-in-a-lifetime, life-changing event – often one that has been fought for and been a long time coming.

I was surprised by the grip IVF and loss continued to have on my life even after giving birth to Percy. I was anxious for the majority of his first year. Gradually, over time, my fear that he would be taken away from me has lessened, but I think the notion may always be there, niggling away in the background. I have already lost something so precious, so I know all too well how painful it is to say goodbye to a child.

Leaving Percy to return to work was a challenge. I had spent so long wishing him into existence that it felt wrong to be leaving him in the care of someone else, however trusted they might be. Having returned to work, at a different hospital, I have fallen in love with midwifery all over again. Just as having Cecil and Wilfred influenced how I work as a midwife, having Percy has done the same. For me, experiencing loss and infertility has really helped me understand how to be compassionate in my profession. I feel strongly that midwives do not have to have experienced pregnancy or birth to be excellent practitioners, but having the ability to be empathetic is something that makes a midwife stand out.

NHS midwives continue to work in challenging conditions. Working long hours, often staying late, having no breaks and sometimes working twelve-hour shifts without eating, drinking or even going to the toilet are all normal. The physical demands are immense, but the mental load is heavier. There is the volume of things to remember, having to make sure every 't' is crossed and every 'i' is dotted, the fear of litigation, the fear of losing your livelihood and your passion because of a mistake. And then there is the emotional toll on top of that. Having to care for families during the most harrowing experiences, resuscitating babies, stopping major haemorrhages, rushing to theatre for crash deliveries, and then going home to sleep for a few hours before returning to do it all over again. There is little time to properly process or acknowledge the fraught situations we have lived through.

I am so very thankful to every midwife who helped carry me through my pregnancies. I am proud to stand alongside some of the most inspiring colleagues.

Despite the crisis within the NHS, there still needs to be a focus on the changes that can be made to help improve the experiences of patients. As I talked about earlier, one of those is the use of language. There are many standard terms and phrases within maternity services that range from the ill-informed to the insulting. Women and birthing people need to be put at the centre of any discussion about their own health, and using inclusive, appropriate language is vital. I try to educate my colleagues when I hear language that I find unhelpful; however, one person in one hospital cannot change a whole system. Instead, there needs to be a re-evaluation of the language used on a much wider scale, with bodies like the Royal College of Obstetricians & Gynaecologists, the Royal College of Midwives and the National Institute for Health and Care Excellence leading the way to initiate a systemic change.

In the meantime, I will continue to practise what I preach and speak loudly on behalf of women who have experienced infertility and loss. One thing I am often asked is how to support a friend going through this. Firstly, thank you for taking the time to try to understand all they are going through. People are very much individuals and there is no right way to support someone, but my advice would be to take your cue from them. Don't try to find silver linings – just be there.

If you have to share your wonderful news of a pregnancy with someone you know is struggling to bring home a baby, I would encourage you to do this via text message. Pregnancy announcements face to face can be one of the hardest things to encounter. Not because the person in question isn't happy for you – they most definitely will be. But they will also be devastatingly sad for themselves, and the entangling of these opposing feelings in the same moment can be overwhelming to say the least.

Finally, if you are navigating your way through infertility or loss, or both, yourself, I want to let you know that I see you. I see you getting up every day, carrying on while the weight of the world is on your shoulders. There seems to me nothing quite so painful as the yearning for a baby – for one that has not been brought into existence yet, or for one that didn't get to stay.

I know I did everything within my power to become a mother. I fought with every ounce of my being, and that fire lives on as I endeavour to provide some words of support to those still wading through the mud.

I don't feel like I have my happily ever after, because it is impossible to feel that way knowing that two very special boys are missing from my life. Phrases like 'it was all worth it in the end' are not easy to face. There is nothing that was worth losing my two eldest sons for. I cannot choose one child over another, so instead I choose to embrace what I do have. The simple moments, like holding my little boy's hand, hearing his laugh or watching his eyes light up when he sees a tractor, of all things, are hard won and precious.

Acknowledgments

It feels quite surreal writing this section of the book, as I can't actually believe this has happened, but there are many people who have helped me along the way.

Firstly thank you to my agent Sallyanne Sweeney. I would never have been brave enough to put pen to paper without your encouragement. I appreciate all the help you gave me, from putting together a proposal and first drafts to making me realise that I did actually have it in me to write a book.

Thank you to Sarah Thickett, my editor, for taking such good care of this book. The subject matter is so very personal, and you have respected and honoured this in such a way that meant I felt confident to share this with the world.

Thank you to the whole team at Hardie Grant. I loved being part of this all-female team, who have been so enthusiastic. I especially loved when I was referred to as 'the author' or 'the writer' as I often forgot that was me!

Thank you to my family for loving and honouring Cecil and Wilfred in ways that will never cease to make me smile.

Thank you to my husband James. Firstly for being such a wonderful support, not only through the book writing process, but also for being such a wonderful partner in life. We've had so much thrown our way, but I know there isn't anything we can't tackle together.

To Percy, thank you for turning the sunshine back on in my life, and for giving me a reason to smile.

To Cecil and Wilfred, the two boys who made me a mother. Never further than my next thought.

Resources

The Miscarriage Association
An organisation supporting families who have experienced miscarriage, molar pregnancy or ectopic pregnancies.
miscarriageassociation.org.uk

Tommy's
A pregnancy charity dedicated to research into pregnancy complications and preventing pregnancy loss.
tommys.org

Sands
The Stillbirth and Neonatal Death Society supports anyone affected by the death of a baby.
sands.org.uk

Twins Trust Bereavement Service
A branch of the Twins Trust specifically aimed at parents who have lost one or more babies during a multiple pregnancy.
twinstrust.org/bereavement

Remember My Baby

A charity providing remembrance photography to families whose baby has died.

remembermybaby.org.uk

Saying Goodbye

A branch of The Mariposa Trust that offers advice, support and more to anyone who has experienced the loss of a baby at any stage.

sayinggoodbye.org

The Lullaby Trust

Support to families who have suffered an unexpected bereavement of a baby or young child.

lullabytrust.org.uk/bereavement-support/

ARC

Antenatal Results and Choices is a charity that provides impartial advice and support for parents during the antenatal screening process.

arc-uk.org

About the Author

Sophie Martin (@the.infertile.midwife) is a registered midwife who worked in a London hospital for ten years before moving to a hospital in Essex. Sophie's wider experience of infertility and baby loss informs her practice, and has led to her being approached by organisations such as Emma's Diary and My Surrogacy Journey to provide a professional overview. Every October, Sophie curates and delivers a series of online talks and interviews to coincide with Baby Loss Awareness Week, during which she's been in conversation with guests such as Elizabeth Day and Izzy Judd. Sophie lives in Essex with her husband and young son.